A KEY TO THE

CASELESS CADDIS LARVAE OF THE BRITISH ISLES

with notes on their ecology

by

J. M. EDINGTON*
and
A. G. HILDREW†

FRESHWATER BIOLOGICAL ASSOCIATION
SCIENTIFIC PUBLICATION No. 43

1981

* Department of Zoology, University College, University of Wales, Cardiff, CF1 1XL.
† Department of Zoology and Comparative Physiology, Queen Mary College, University of London, Mile End Road, London, E1 4NS.

PREFACE

Over the last few years the Association has been working towards filling the two remaining major gaps in the availability of keys for the identification of British freshwater macro-invertebrates. These gaps have been the Chironomidae and the Trichoptera. With the publication in 1973 of Dr Macan's key (*FBA Scientific Publication No. 28*) identification of the adults of the Trichoptera became possible. Dr Pinder's key to the adult Chironomidae (*FBA Scientific Publication No. 37, 1978*) provided a similar service for students of the chironomids. However, the larvae of both groups remained stumbling blocks for those working with freshwater insects. Now, the publication of this key to caseless caddis larvae makes a start in overcoming this situation. We are grateful to Dr Edington and his past student, Dr Hildrew, for preparing this key. Both have spent much of their working lives studying caddis larvae and so are well fitted to write this handbook.

With this key, we have also continued a recent development in the series, which is to include not only a taxonomic guide but also notes summarizing present knowledge about the natural history of the animals concerned. Thus, in the present handbook, the key itself and the taxonomic notes are followed by sections on feeding biology, habitat distribution and life history. Caseless caddis larvae often spin characteristic and elaborate nets to catch their prey so it is appropriate that there should be a section describing this and other feeding habits. As the authors point out (on page 69), at this stage of knowledge about caddis larvae, distribution maps would be of limited value, so such maps have not been included in this key. Indeed, it has become apparent that only for very well researched groups does the publication of distribution maps for freshwater animals warrant the considerable labour involved in their preparation.

The Ferry House   E. D. Le Cren
January 1981.   *Director*

ISBN 0900386 41 X
ISSN 0367-1887

CONTENTS

INTRODUCTION

To most people the word "caddis" conjures up a picture of an aquatic insect living inside a transportable case which it has constructed from sand particles, small stones or plant fragments. Indeed, it has been suggested (Hickin 1967) that the word caddis may derive from the habit once practised by travelling salesmen of pinning samples of braid and ribbons or "cadace" to their coats. It is less generally known that there are substantial numbers of caddis larvae (47 species are listed for Britain) which never make transportable cases. Some (the Hydropsychidae, Polycentropodidae and Philopotamidae) are associated with silk nets (Figs 127–137) which they use to collect food, others (the Psychomyiidae) live principally within meandering galleries constructed on rock surfaces (Plate 1b), and the members of one family (the Rhyacophilidae) are freely-moving predators.

Our treatment of this somewhat diverse assemblage falls into two sections. In the first section (p. 11) we have provided, in the form of a key and an associated taxonomic commentary, the information necessary to identify caseless caddis species. In the second section (p. 60) we have summarized the information currently available on various aspects of the ecology and general biology of the group. This latter account deals with feeding biology, habitat distribution and life histories. With these families, as with others, detailed ecological studies were able to get under way only when the taxonomic problems had been resolved; a point worth stressing when taxonomic work seems to have fallen out of fashion.

It might seem a very straightforward matter to distinguish caddis larvae with cases from those without them. Unfortunately, however, the process of collection, particularly by means of a net or other sampling device, frequently separates cased caddis from their cases. Similarly net-spinners become separated from their nets and gallery-builders from their galleries. In the probable absence of such clues, the key has to deal initially with both cased and caseless larvae and to distinguish between them on the basis of morphological features. Further identification of cased larvae to species level will become possible when the appropriate key is completed.

In the framework of the present key the family Hydroptilidae presents a complication because its members construct cases in the 5th (final) instar but not in the earlier stages. Fortunately for our purpose, the early stages are of short duration, probably lasting only about four weeks in total (Nielsen 1948) and are rarely encountered in the field.   Consequently we have felt justified in not complicating the key by attempting to cater for them.

There are some differences of opinion about the subdivision of the Trichoptera into families.   Here we have adopted the prevailing view (Lepneva 1970, Wiggins 1977) that the Glossosomatidae should be separated from the Rhyacophilidae.   Also we are persuaded by the arguments of Lepneva (1956, 1970) that the larvae and pupae of *Ecnomus* are sufficiently distinct from those of the Psychomyiidae to warrant the separation of this genus into a separate family, the Ecnomidae.   In these respects the arrangement of families adopted here differs from that used in the well-known check list provided by Kimmins (1966).

CHECKLIST OF CASELESS CADDIS IN THE BRITISH ISLES
(redundant specific names are shown in parentheses)

RHYACOPHILIDAE
RHYACOPHILA Pictet, 1834
1   *dorsalis* (Curtis, 1834)
2   *septentrionis* McLachlan, 1865
3   *obliterata* McLachlan, 1865
4   *munda* McLachlan, 1862

PHILOPOTAMIDAE
PHILOPOTAMUS Stephens, 1829
5   *montanus* (Donovan, 1813)
WORMALDIA McLachlan, 1865
6   *occipitalis* (Pictet, 1834)
7   *mediana* McLachlan, 1878
8   *subnigra* McLachlan, 1865
CHIMARRA Stephens, 1829
9   *marginata* (L., 1758)

POLYCENTROPODIDAE
NEURECLIPSIS McLachlan, 1864
10   *bimaculata* (L., 1758)

PLECTROCNEMIA Stephens, 1836
11 *conspersa* (Curtis, 1834)
12 *geniculata* McLachlan, 1871
*13 *brevis* McLachlan, 1871
POLYCENTROPUS Curtis, 1835
14 *flavomaculatus* (Pictet, 1834)
15 *irroratus* (Curtis, 1835)
      (*multiguttatus*)
16 *kingi* McLachlan, 1881
HOLOCENTROPUS McLachlan, 1878
17 *dubius* (Rambur, 1842)
18 *picicornis* (Stephens, 1836)
19 *stagnalis* (Albarda, 1874)
CYRNUS Stephens, 1836
20 *trimaculatus* (Curtis, 1834)
21 *insolutus* McLachlan, 1878
22 *flavidus* McLachlan, 1864

ECNOMIDAE
ECNOMUS McLachlan, 1864
23 *tenellus* (Rambur, 1842)

PSYCHOMYIIDAE
TINODES Leach, 1815
24 *waeneri* (L., 1758)
25 *maclachlani* Kimmins, 1966
      (*aureolus*)
      (*pusillus*)
26 *assimilis* McLachlan, 1865
27 *pallidulus* McLachlan, 1878
28 *maculicornis* (Pictet, 1834)
29 *unicolor* (Pictet, 1834)
30 *rostocki* McLachlan, 1878
31 *dives* (Pictet, 1834)
LYPE McLachlan, 1878
32 *phaeopa* (Stephens, 1836)
33 *reducta* (Hagen, 1860)
METALYPE Klapálek, 1898
34 *fragilis* (Pictet, 1834)

* the current status of this species in the British Isles is uncertain.

PSYCHOMYIA Latreille, 1829
35 *pusilla* (Fabr., 1781)

HYDROPSYCHIDAE
HYDROPSYCHE Pictet, 1834
36 *pellucidula* (Curtis, 1834)
37 *angustipennis* (Curtis, 1834)
38 *saxonica* McLachlan, 1884
39 *contubernalis* McLachlan, 1865
     (*ornatula*)
*40 *guttata* Pictet, 1834
41   *siltalai* Döhler, 1963
     (*instabilis*)
42   *instabilis* (Curtis, 1834)
     (*fulvipes*)
43   *fulvipes* (Curtis, 1834)
*44 *exocellata* Dufour, 1841
*45 *bulgaromanorum* Malicky, 1977
         CHEUMATOPSYCHE Wallengren, 1891
46   *lepida* (Pictet, 1834)
         DIPLECTRONA Westwood, 1840
47   *felix* McLachlan, 1878

In compiling the present key we have made use of existing keys but have modified them in the light of new information, and also difficulties encountered in their use.   The principal sources are as follows:

Polycentropodidae: Edington (1964)

Hydropsychidae: Hildrew & Morgan (1974) and incorporating the posterior prosternite characters suggested by Boon (1978b)

Psychomyiidae: Edington & Alderson (1973) modified to accommodate the newly discovered larva of *Tinodes maculicornis* (Pictet) described by O'Connor & Wise (1980)

Rhyacophilidae: Mackereth (1954) and incorporating the additional pronotum characters suggested by Hickin (1954)

* the current status of these species in the British Isles is uncertain.

Inevitably a few problems still remain. It has not been possible to include species such as *Plectrocnemia brevis* McLach., *Hydropsyche guttata* Pictet or *Hydropsyche exocellata* Dufour. These have not been found in Britain since the beginning of the century and their larvae have never been described. Neither have we been able to devise an effective means of separating the larvae of the three *Wormaldia* species. The situation here has been complicated by a revision of the adult taxonomy (Kimmins 1965) which has made it difficult to interpret earlier records and larval descriptions.

It is hoped that users of this key will participate in making good these deficiencies and any others which emerge.

The handbook by Macan (1973) is the most appropriate general work to use in identifying caddis adults. However this should be replaced by Hildrew & Morgan (1974) when dealing with the Hydropsychidae, because this latter work takes account of the recent taxonomic revision of the family (Tobias 1972a, b). Also the new key by Marshall (1978) supersedes the section in Macan's handbook dealing with the Hydroptilidae. Fisher (1977) has provided additional information on the adult females of the genus *Tinodes* (Psychomyiidae).

PRESERVATION AND EXAMINATION

Larvae for taxonomic investigation are usually preserved in 70 or 80% ethyl or isopropyl alcohol, although some taxonomists prefer more complex fixatives such as Kahle's or Pampel's fluids (see below) because they penetrate the specimen more rapidly and are also more effective in preserving green and yellow colours.

Composition of preservatives (parts by volume)

	Kahle's fluid	Pampel's fluid
Ethyl alcohol	15	15
Distilled water	30	30
Formalin	6	6
Glacial acetic acid	1	4

Whilst the mixed fixatives certainly have the advantages claimed for them, we found in the case of psychomyiid larvae that Pampel's fluid caused fading of the taxonomically-important pigment patches on the underside of the thorax.

Most of the characters used in the key should be visible using a binocular microscope at ×50 magnification. Where it is appropriate to mount a part on a microscope slide for examination at higher magnifications, polyvinyl lactophenol or Berlese's fluid are recommended as suitable temporary

mountants.   The most convenient way of producing a permanent mount is
to immerse the specimen in glacial acetic acid for 5 minutes, transfer it to
clove oil for at least 15 minutes and then mount it in Canada balsam.

NOTES ON USE OF THE KEY

Finally some comments about the use of the key; we have included in the
couplets what seem to be the most obvious and useful features, and in the
first instance the specimen in question should be run straight through the
key on this basis.   When a provisional answer has been obtained, the
taxonomic commentary (p. 47) appropriate to that family should be read
carefully.   This will provide additional taxonomic features, warn of
problems of variability of characters and their application to early instar
larvae, and also mention life history features or distribution patterns of
potential diagnostic value.   This additional information should be
sufficient to confirm the original identification or to cast doubt on it.   In the
latter case another excursion through the key is indicated.

THE KEY

1   1st abdominal segment carries structures for supporting a case, which may take one of the following forms:
(a) Three fleshy protuberances, one dorsal, two lateral (Figs 2–4)—
case bearer: Families PHRYGANEIDAE, LIMNEPHILIDAE, MOLANNIDAE, BERAEIDAE, ODONTOCERIDAE, GOERIDAE.
(b) One dorsal protuberance, two lateral, plate-like pads (Figs 5–7)—
case bearer: Families LEPTOCERIDAE, SERICOSTOMATIDAE.
(c) Lateral fleshy protuberances only (Fig. 8)—
case bearer: Family LEPIDOSTOMATIDAE.

—   None of these case-supporting structures is present on 1st abdominal segment—   **2**

2   Distinct hard plates present on dorsal surface of 2nd and 3rd thoracic segments (Figs 20–24)—   **7**

—   No plates on dorsal surface of 2nd and 3rd thoracic segments (Figs 15–19)—   **3**

3   Tufted gills present on abdominal segments (Fig. 15)—
Family RHYACOPHILIDAE (taxonomic notes, p. 47) **11**

—   No tufted gills on abdominal segments (Figs 16–19)—   **4**

4   Labrum principally composed of a transverse sclerotized plate* (Figs 10–12)—   **5**

—   Labrum neither sclerotized nor plate-like, but white and membranous with brush-like anterior border (Fig. 9)—
Family PHILOPOTAMIDAE (taxonomic notes, p. 47) **14**

---

* It is important to ensure that it is the labrum which is being examined and not the front margin of the head; sometimes the labrum is retracted and needs to be drawn forward for examination.

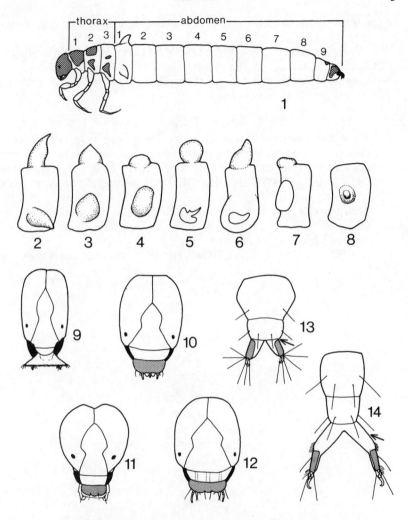

Figs 1–14. 1: generalized diagram of caddis larva to show segmentation.
2–8: lateral views of 1st abdominal segment in various families (anterior to left): 2 – Phryganeidae; 3 – Limnephilidae; 4 – Beraeidae; 5, 6 – Leptoceridae; 7 – Sericostomatidae; 8 – Lepidostomatidae.
9–12: head capsules, dorsal: 9 – Philopotamidae; 10 – Psychomyiidae; 11 – *Glossosoma* (Glossosomatidae); 12 – Polycentropodidae.
13: anal prolegs, Psychomyiidae.
14: anal prolegs, Polycentropodidae.

5 Lateral plates on 2nd and 3rd thoracic segments large and obvious
(Fig. 16)—
case bearer: Family GLOSSOSOMATIDAE (Genus GLOSSOSOMA)

— Lateral plates on 2nd and 3rd thoracic segments small and inconspicuous (Figs 17–19)— **6**

6 Basal membranous section of each anal proleg (Fig. 18, arrow *a*;
Fig. 14, arrow) equal in length to distal sclerotized section. Under-
sides of femora with numerous long bristles (Fig. 18, arrow *b*)—
Family POLYCENTROPODIDAE (taxonomic notes, p. 48) **16**

— Anal prolegs have virtually no basal membranous section (Fig. 17,
arrow *a*, Fig. 13 arrow). Undersides of femora with only a few
isolated bristles (Fig. 17, arrow *b*)—
Family PSYCHOMYIIDAE (taxonomic notes, p. 51) **27**

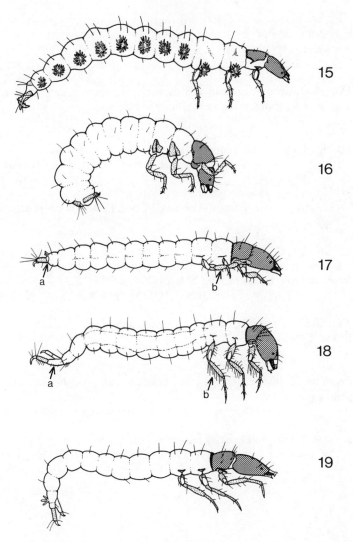

Figs 15–19.   Typical larvae of various families: 15 – Rhyacophilidae; 16 – *Glossosoma* (Glossosomatidae); 17 – Psychomyiidae; 18 – Polycentropodidae; 19 – Philopotamidae.

7(2) Dorsal plates on 2nd and 3rd thoracic segments large and rectangular and similar in size to plates on 1st thoracic segment (Figs
22–24)—   **9**

— Dorsal plates on 2nd and 3rd thoracic segments much smaller than
plates on 1st thoracic segment (Figs 20–21)—   **8**

8 1st leg much shorter than 2nd and 3rd legs (Fig. 20)—
                            case bearer: Family BRACHYCENTRIDAE*

— 1st leg as long as 2nd and 3rd legs (Fig. 21)—
              case bearer: Family GLOSSOSOMATIDAE (Genus AGAPETUS)

9(7) Tufted gills present on abdominal segments (Fig. 22), anal prolegs
have terminal brush of long bristles (Fig. 22)—
                   Family HYDROPSYCHIDAE (taxonomic notes, p. 55) **38**

— No tufted gills on abdominal segments, anal prolegs without terminal
brush (Figs 23, 24)—   **10**

10 Prominent lateral fringe of bristles on abdominal segments
(Fig. 23—   Family ECNOMIDAE
            (taxonomic notes, p. 59) **Ecnomus tenellus** (Rambur)

— No lateral fringe of bristles on abdominal segments (Fig. 24)—
                  case bearer: Family HYDROPTILIDAE (5th instar)

* The only British species, *Brachycentrus subnubilis* Curtis is distinguishable by its dorsal
abdominal gills (Fig. 20). However, this is not necessarily the case with brachycentrid
larvae elsewhere.

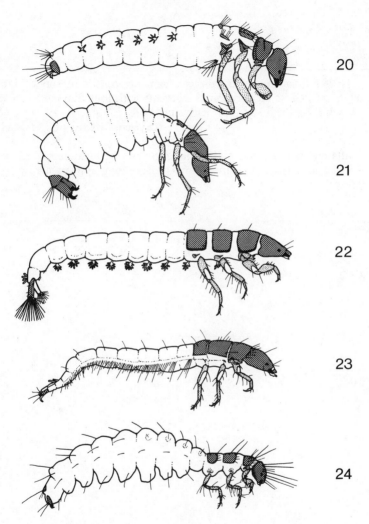

Figs 20–24. Typical larvae of various families: 20 – Brachycentridae; 21 – *Agapetus* (Glossosomatidae); 22 – Hydropsychidae; 23 – Ecnomidae; 24 – Hydroptilidae.

11(3) Gills on 2nd and 3rd thoracic segments consist of single filament
(Fig. 25), those on abdominal segments with four filaments (Fig. 26).
Auxiliary spine on anal prolegs, short (Fig. 28, arrow)—
Rhyacophila munda McLachlan

— Gills on thoracic and abdominal segments with numerous filaments
(Fig. 27).   Auxiliary spine on anal prolegs, long (Fig. 29, arrow)— **12**

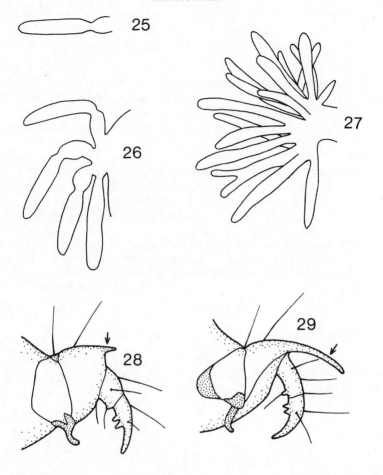

Figs 25–29. *Rhyacophila:*
25: thoracic gill of *R. munda*; 26: abdominal gills of *R. munda*; 27: thoracic gills of *R. dorsalis*; (Figs 25-27 after Mackereth 1954). 28: anal claw and auxiliary spine of *R. munda*; 29: anal claw and auxiliary spine of *R. septentrionis*.

12   Head with straight and almost parallel sides (Fig. 31)—
                           Rhyacophila obliterata McLachlan

—   Head with rounded sides, tapering anteriorly (Figs 32, 33)—   **13**

13   Dorsal posterior region of head has conspicuous pattern of dark spots
     on a lighter background (Fig. 33, arrow *a*).   Pigment on pronotum in
     three separate areas, one median and two lateral (Fig. 35)—
                           Rhyacophila septentrionis McLachlan

—   Dorsal posterior region of head darkly and diffusely pigmented with-
     out conspicuous pattern of dark spots (Fig. 32, arrow *a*).   Pigment
     on pronotum forms a small continuous area with an irregular outline
     (Fig. 34)—   **Rhyacophila dorsalis** (Curtis)

Figs 30–35.   *Rhyacophila:*
                30: head capsule, dorsal of *R. munda*; 31: head capsule, dorsal of *R. obliterata*;
                32: head capsule, dorsal of *R. dorsalis*; 33: head capsule, dorsal of
                R. septentrionis; (Figs 30–33 after Mackereth 1954).   34: pronotum of
                R. dorsalis; 35: pronotum of *R. septentrionis*; (Figs 34 & 35 after Hickin 1954).

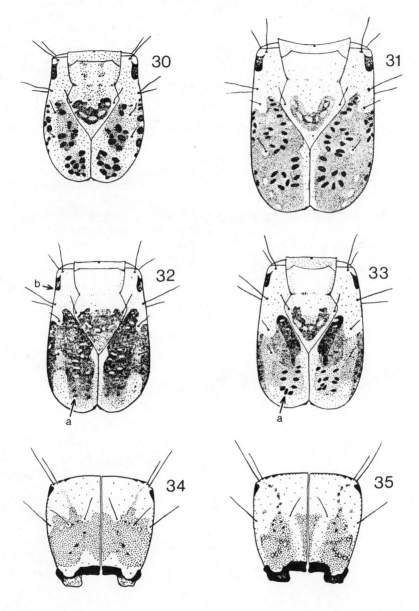

14(4) Anterior margin of frontoclypeus has smooth outline (Fig. 36)—
Genus WORMALDIA (see p. 48)

—   Anterior margin of frontoclypeus notched—   **15**

15   Notch in frontoclypeus deep and 'U' shaped (Fig. 37)—
Chimarra marginata (L.)

—   Notch in frontoclypeus shallow and roughly 'V' shaped (Fig. 38)—
Philopotamus montanus (Donovan)

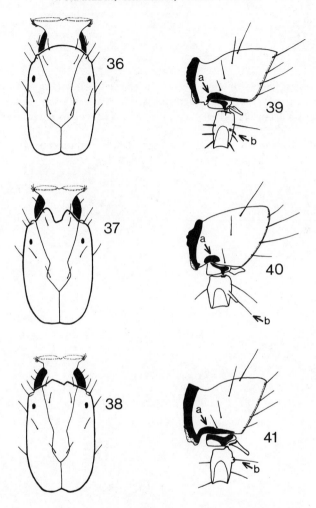

Figs 36–41. 36: head capsule, dorsal of *Wormaldia*; 37: head capsule, dorsal of *Chimarra marginata*; 38: head capsule, dorsal of *Philopotamus montanus*; 39–41: lateral views of pronota and front coxae of philopotamid larvae (anterior to right: 39 – *Wormaldia*; 40 – *Chimarra marginata*; 41 – *Philopotamus montanus*.

16(6) Basal segment of anal prolegs without bristles (Fig. 42, arrow *a*). Ventral surface of 9th abdominal segment bears a pair of stout spines (Figs 42, arrow *b*, 43)—   **Neureclipsis bimaculata** (L.)

— Basal segment of anal prolegs bears numerous bristles. 9th abdominal segment without stout ventral spines—   **17**

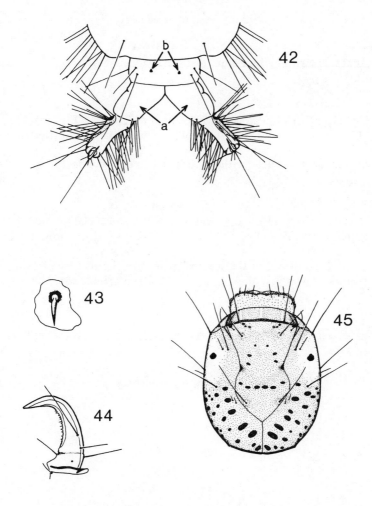

Figs 42–45. *Neureclipsis bimaculata:*
42: anal prolegs, ventral (*a* – basal segment, *b* – ventral spine); 43: ventral spine; 44: anal claw, lateral; 45: head capsule, dorsal.

17   Anal claws with four blunt teeth on inside edge (Fig. 46)—
                                           Genus CYRNUS, **18**

—   Anal claws without four blunt teeth on inside edge—   **20**

18   Dorsal surface of head with conspicuous dark bands (Fig. 47)—
                                           Cyrnus trimaculatus (Curtis)

—   Dorsal surface of head without conspicuous dark bands (Figs 48, 49)—
                                                                        19

19   Central light area on the frontoclypeus includes some spots in the
      posterior row (Fig. 48)—   **Cyrnus flavidus** McLachlan

—   Central light area on the frontoclypeus does not include spots in the
      posterior row (Fig. 49)—   **Cyrnus insolutus** McLachlan

20(17) Tarsus (Fig. 50, ta) of 1st leg less than half length of tibia (Fig.
      50, ti)—   Genus POLYCENTROPUS, **21**

—   Tarsus of 1st leg about same length as tibia (Fig. 51)—   **23**

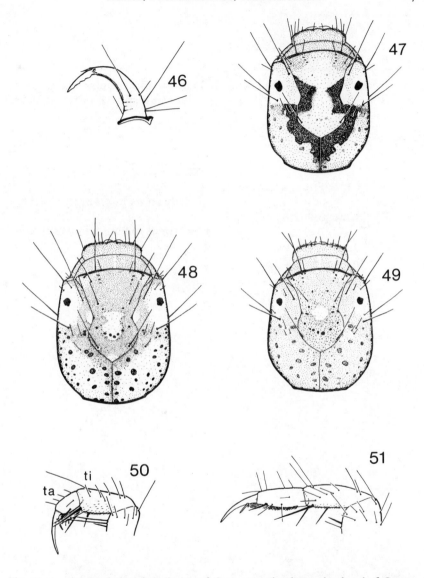

Figs 46–51. 46: anal claw, lateral view of *Cyrnus*; 47: head capsule, dorsal of *Cyrnus trimaculatus*; 48: head capsule, dorsal of *Cyrnus flavidus*; 49: head capsule, dorsal of *Cyrnus insolutus*; 50: tibia and tarsus of 1st leg of *Polycentropus*; 51: tibia and tarsus of 1st leg of *Plectrocnemia*.

21   Dorsal surface of head without marked discontinuities of pigment
     (Fig. 52)—   **Polycentropus irroratus** (Curtis)

—   Dorsal surface of head with marked discontinuities of pigment
     (Figs 53–55)—   **22**

22   Anal claws obtuse-angled (Fig. 56)—
                                     Polycentropus kingi McLachlan
—   Anal claws right-angled (Fig. 57)—
                              Polycentropus flavomaculatus (Pictet)

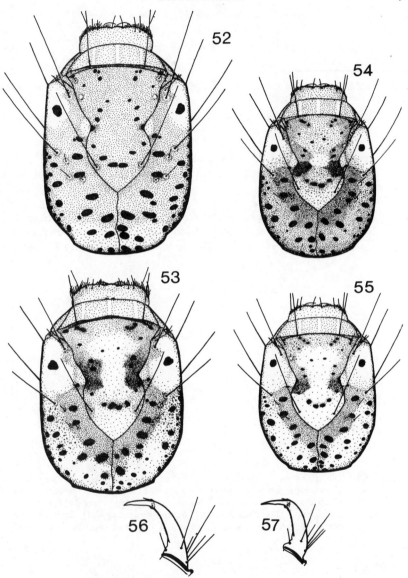

Figs 52–57. *Polycentropus:*
52: head capsule, dorsal of *P. irroratus*; 53: head capsule, dorsal of *P. kingi*; 54, 55: head capsule, dorsal of *P. flavomaculatus*; 56: anal claw of *P. kingi*; 57: anal claw of *P. flavomaculatus*.

23(20) Anal claws obtuse-angled (Fig. 58)——   Genus PLECTROCNEMIA, **24**

——   Anal claws right-angled (Fig. 59)——   Genus HOLOCENTROPUS, **25**

24   Bristles on ventral side of last abdominal segment numerous (Fig. 60). Median pigment mark present on posterior margin of labrum (Fig. 61)——   **Plectrocnemia conspersa** (Curtis)

——   Bristles on ventral side of last abdominal segment sparse (Fig. 62). No median pigment mark on posterior margin of labrum (Fig. 63)——   **Plectrocnemia geniculata** McLachlan

Figs 58–66.   58: anal claw of *Plectrocnemia*; 59: anal claw of *Holocentropus*; 60: 9th abdominal segment, ventral of *Plectrocnemia conspersa*; 61: labrum, dorsal of *Plectrocnemia conspersa*; 62: 9th abdominal segment, ventral of *Plectrocnemia geniculata*; 63: labrum, dorsal of *Plectrocnemia geniculata*; 64: head capsule, dorsal of *Plectrocnemia geniculata*; 65, 66: head capsule, dorsal of *Plectrocnemia conspersa*.

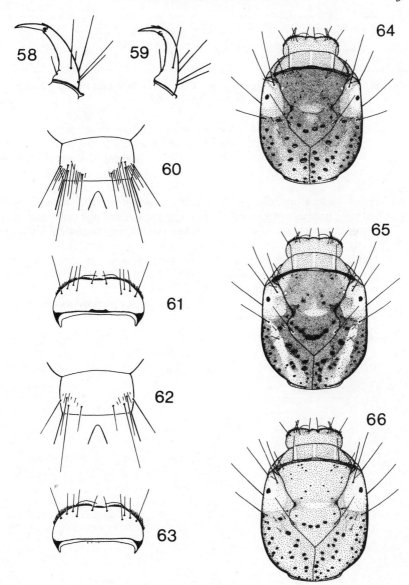

25(23) Dorsal surface of head with dark bands of pigmentation and pale
       median stripe on frontoclypeus (Figs 67, 68)—   **26**

—   Dorsal surface of head without distinct dark bands of pigmentation.
       No continuous median stripe on frontoclypeus (Fig. 69)—
                                        Holocentropus dubius (Rambur)

26   Head broad and short.   Pale median stripe on frontoclypeus clouded
       with pigment at anterior end.   No light areas alongside constriction of
       frontoclypeus (Fig. 67)—   **Holocentropus stagnalis** (Albarda)

—   Head narrow and elongate.   Pale median stripe on frontoclypeus
       clear of pigment at its anterior end.   Light areas present alongside
       constriction of frontoclypeus (Fig. 68)—
                                        Holocentropus picicornis (Stephens)

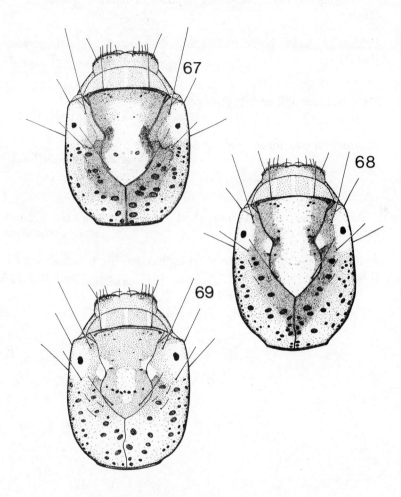

Figs 67–69. Head capsules of *Holocentropus*: 67 – *H. stagnalis*; 68 – *H. picicornis*; 69 – *H. dubius*.

27(6) Pronotum has black thickening in posterior-lateral position (Fig. 70 arrow)—   **28**

— Pronotum lacks black thickening in posterior-lateral position (Fig. 71)—   **29**

28 Mentum black and heavily ornamented (Fig. 72)
                                                    Psychomyia pusilla (Fabr.)

— Mentum brown, smooth and not ornamented (Fig. 73)
                                                    Metalype fragilis (Pictet)

29(27) Anterior part of coxopleurite* of 1st leg has two vertical black bars (Fig. 77 arrows)—   Genus TINODES, **31**

— Anterior part of coxopleurite of 1st leg has only one vertical black bar (Fig. 78 arrow)—   Genus LYPE, **30**

* The coxopleurites are small plates above the leg bases.

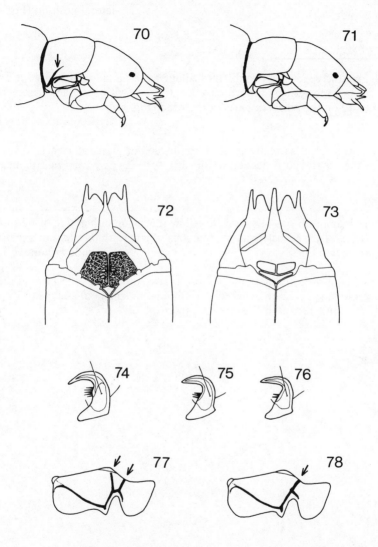

Figs 70–78.   70: lateral view of head and thorax of *Psychomyia*; 71: lateral view of head and thorax of *Tinodes*; 72: head, ventral to show mentum, *Psychomyia pusilla*; 73: head, ventral to show mentum, *Metalype fragilis*; 74: anal claw of *Psychomyia pusilla*; 75, 76: anal claw of *Metalype fragilis*; 77: 1st coxopleurite of *Tinodes* (anterior to right); 78: 1st coxopleurite of *Lype* (anterior to right).

30   Frontoclypeus has two distinct colour zones; a pale anterior zone and
      a dark posterior zone which is continuous with the dark transverse
      band on the adjacent parts of the head (Fig. 79)—

                                                Lype reducta (Hagen)

—   Frontoclypeus relatively uniform in colour without clearly defined
      anterior and posterior zones (Fig. 80)—   **Lype phaeopa** (Stephens)

31(29) Pronotum has large ovoid yellow marks on either side of mid-line
      (Fig. 84); frontoclypeus conspicuously darker than adjacent areas of
      the head (Fig. 85)—   **Tinodes waeneri** (L.)

—   Pronotum without ovoid yellow marks on either side of mid-line;
      frontoclypeus not markedly different in pigment intensity from
      adjacent areas of the head (Figs 89, 90, 95–97)—   **32**

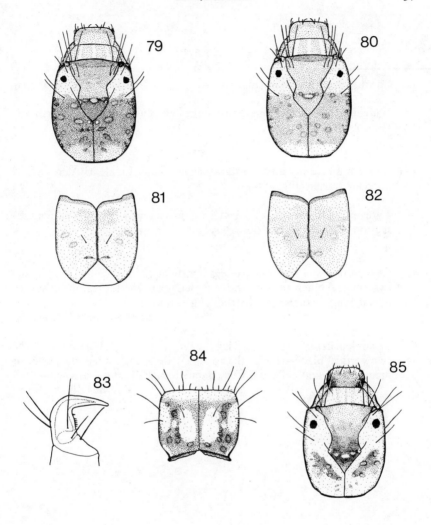

Figs 79–82. Head capsules of *Lype*: 79 – *L. reducta*, dorsal; 80 – *L. phaeopa*, dorsal; 81 – *L. reducta*, ventral; 82 – *L. phaeopa*, ventral.

Figs 83–85. *Tinodes waeneri*: 83 – anal claw; 84 – pronotum, dorsal; 85 – head capsule, dorsal.

32   Labrum uniformly pale (Fig. 86)—   **Tinodes unicolor** (Pictet)

—   Labrum with dark pigmentation either evenly or unevenly distributed
      (Figs 87, 88)—   **33**

33   Labrum uniformly black or dark brown except for clearly demarcated
      anterior margin (Fig. 87)—   **34**

—   Labrum pigmentation of uneven intensity and with greatest concen-
      tration around the posterior lateral points (Fig. 88)—   **35**

34   Coxopleurites of 2nd and 3rd legs lightly pigmented (Fig. 91). Of the
      two vertical black arms on the coxopleurite of the 1st leg, the posterior
      arm is long, and sharply defined (Fig. 93, arrow)—
                                              Tinodes rostocki McLachlan

—   Coxopleurites of 2nd and 3rd legs heavily pigmented (Fig. 92). Of the
      two vertical black arms on the coxopleurite of the 1st leg, the posterior
      arm is short and ends in diffuse pigmentation (Fig. 94, arrow)—
                                                  Tinodes dives (Pictet)

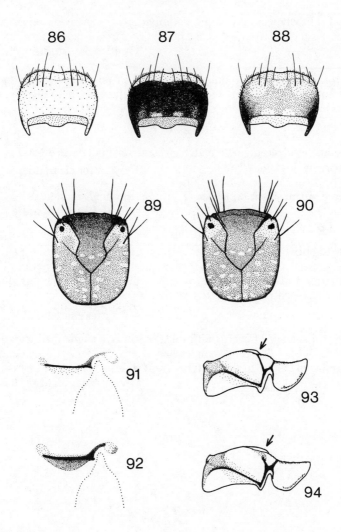

Figs 86–94. *Tinodes:*
86: labrum of *T. unicolor*; 87: labrum of *T. dives*; 88: labrum of *T. assimilis*;
89: head capsule of *T. dives*; 90: head capsule of *T. unicolor*; 91: 2nd
coxopleurite of *T. rostocki*, anterior to right (head of coxa shown by dotted
line); 92: 2nd coxopleurite of *T. dives*, anterior to right; 93: 1st coxopleurite of
T. rostocki, anterior to right; 94: 1st coxopleurite of *T. dives*, anterior to right.

35(33) Frontoclypeus has single dominant pale spot in posterior region;
other spots on frontoclypeus and rest of dorsal head surface indistinct
(Fig. 97)—   **Tinodes pallidulus** McLachlan

— Frontoclypeus has 3 similar pale spots in posterior region; spots on
frontoclypeus and rest of dorsal head surface distinct (Figs 95, 96)—
36

36 Reddish-purple pigment patch present on underside of 2nd thoracic
segment (Fig. 98, arrow)—   **37**

— No pigment patch on underside of 2nd thoracic segment—
Tinodes maculicornis (Pictet)

37 Dorsal surface of each anal proleg has a series of 3–5 pale spots
(Fig. 99). On the coxopleurite of the 1st leg, the trochantin (i.e. the
anterior leaf-like structure) is appreciably darker in colour than the
posterior-ventral area (Fig. 101, arrows)—
Tinodes assimilis McLachlan

— Dorsal surface of each anal proleg has only a single distinct pale spot
(Fig. 100). On the coxopleurite of the 1st leg, the trochantin is
similar in colour to the posterior-ventral area (Fig. 102, arrows)—
Tinodes maclachlani Kimmins

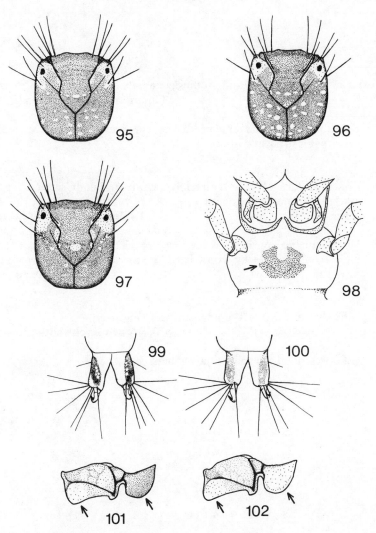

Figs 95–102. *Tinodes:*
95: head capsule of *T. assimilis*; 96: head capsule of *T. maclachlani*; 97: head capsule of *T. pallidulus*; 98: underside of 2nd thoracic segment of *T. maclachlani*, with pigment patch; 99: anal prolegs, dorsal of *T. assimilis*; 100: anal prolegs, dorsal of *T. maclachlani*; 101: 1st coxopleurite, lateral of *T. assimilis*, (anterior to right); 102: 1st coxopleurite, lateral of *T. maclachlani*, (anterior to right).

38(9) Dorsal part of head and prothorax densely covered with long bristles
(Fig. 103)—   **Cheumatopsyche lepida** (Pictet)

—   Dorsal part of head and prothorax not densely covered with long
bristles (Figs 104, 106)—   **39**

39   Dorsal surface of head uniformly brown in colour without yellow
marks.   Frontoclypeus with a marked constriction at about the level
of the eyes (Fig. 105)—   **Diplectrona felix** McLachlan

—   Dorsal surface of head with conspicuous yellow marks.   Frontoclypeus not markedly constricted at the level of the eyes (Figs
121–126)—   Genus HYDROPSYCHE, **40**

40   Gills absent on 7th abdominal segment (Fig. 107)—
                                            Hydropsyche siltalai Döhler

—   Gills present on 7th abdominal segment (Fig. 108)—   **41**

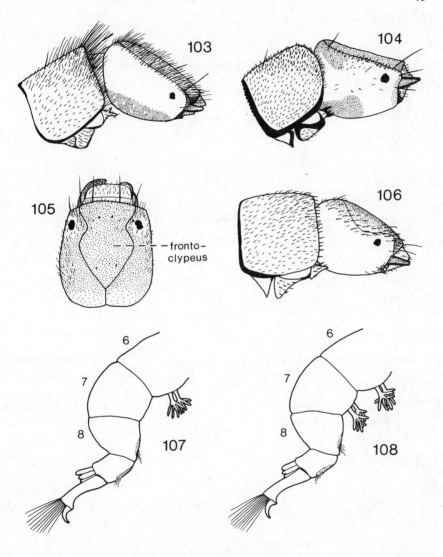

Figs 103–108.   103: head and thorax, lateral of *Cheumatopsyche lepida*; 104: head and thorax, lateral of Genus *Hydropsyche*; 105: head, dorsal of *Diplectrona felix*; 106: head and thorax, lateral of *Diplectrona felix*; 107: posterior of abdomen, lateral, *Hydropsyche siltalai*; 108: posterior of abdomen, lateral, *Hydropsyche* species other than *siltalai*.

41   Posterior prosternites* uniformly pale and indistinct (Fig. 111)—
                Hydropsyche contubernalis McLachlan

—   Posterior prosternites partly or entirely darkly-pigmented (Figs
     112–115)—   **42 (Table)**

42. Table for separation of *Hydropsyche angustipennis, H. pellucidula,*
                    H. instabilis and *H. fulvipes*

	posterior prosternites	mentum	frontoclypeus shape	frontoclypeus marks	
— (a)	lateral parts dark (Fig. 112)	median channel straight-sided, rounded lateral margins (Fig. 118)	V shaped (Fig. 125)	faint or absent posterior mark (Fig. 125)	**Hydropsyche angustipennis** (Curtis)
— (b)	lateral parts light (Fig. 113)	median channel straight-sided, square lateral margins (Fig. 117)	V shaped (Fig. 126)	Y or bar shaped posterior mark (Fig. 126)	**Hydropsyche pellucidula** (Curtis)
— (c)	lateral parts light (Fig. 115)	median channel key-hole shaped (Fig. 119)	U shaped (Fig. 124)	U or V shaped posterior mark (Fig. 124)	**Hydropsyche instabilis** (Curtis)
— (d)	lateral parts light (Fig. 114)	median channel key-hole shaped (Fig. 120)	U shaped (Fig. 123)	lateral and posterior marks fused (Fig. 123)	**Hydropsyche fulvipes** (Curtis)

* The posterior prosternites are small plates on the ventral surface of the prothorax.   Their
position is shown in Fig. 110.   It may be necessary to push aside a fold of cuticle to expose
them.

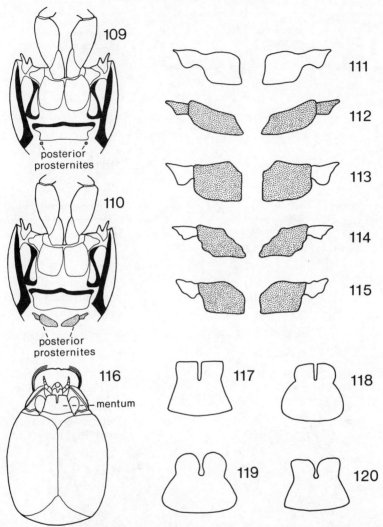

Figs 109–120.　109: underside of 1st thoracic segment to show posterior prosternites, *Cheumatopsyche lepida*.

110: underside of 1st thoracic segment to show posterior prosternites, *Hydropsyche angustipennis*.

111–115: posterior prosternites: 111 – *H. contubernalis*; 112 – *H. angustipennis*; 113 – *H. pellucidula*; 114 – *H. fulvipes*; 115 – *H. instabilis*.

116: ventral surface of head of *Hydropsyche* to show position of mentum.

117–120: mentum shapes: 117 – *H. pellucidula*; 118 – *H. angustipennis*; 119 – *H. instabilis*; 120 – *H. fulvipes*.

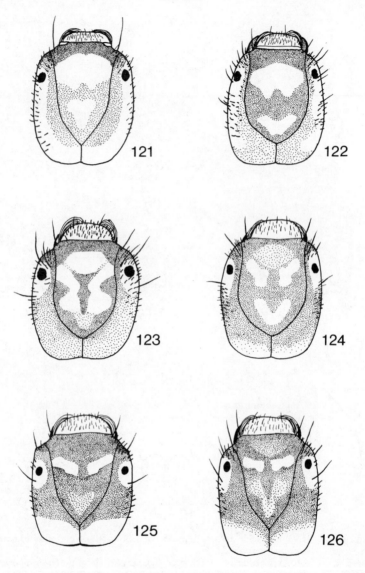

Figs 121–126. Dorsal views of *Hydropsyche* heads: 121 – *H. contubernalis*; 122 – *H. siltalai*; 123 – *H. fulvipes*; 124 – *H. instabilis*; 125 – *H. angustipennis*; 126 – *H. pellucidula*.

TAXONOMIC NOTES

RHYACOPHILIDAE

Rhyacophila munda is readily distinguished from the other *Rhyacophila* species by the arrangement of the gills and the structure of the anal prolegs. In addition the head is markedly constricted in the region of the eyes (Fig. 30). This is more noticeable than in *R. dorsalis* which has the same feature but to a lesser degree (Fig. 32 arrow *b*). In *R. obliterata* the head is straight, almost parallel-sided, and in later instars the frontoclypeus is conspicuously concave at the front (Fig. 31).

The larvae of *R. septentrionis* and *R. dorsalis* can usually be separated satisfactorily using the pigmentation patterns on the head and pronotum. In addition the head is constricted at the level of the eyes in *dorsalis* (Fig. 32, arrow *b*), but not in *septentrionis* (Fig. 33).

R. dorsalis is the commonest of the four *Rhyacophila* species and can be found in the rapids of almost any clean stream or river. The other four species are more localized in their distribution (Mackereth 1954). Mosely (1939) regarded *R. obliterata* as an upland species and subsequent records support this view. Rhyacophilid larvae are freely moving predators (p. 68).

PHILOPOTAMIDAE

The shape of the anterior margin of the frontoclypeus provides a simple method of separating the three genera in the family. When examining this character it may be necessary to push the membranous labrum forward to prevent it from obscuring the anterior margin. Similarly if the mandibles have become reflected inwards care must be taken not to confuse their outline with that of the frontoclypeus.

In addition to this feature, the three genera can be separated by examining the pigmentation of the pronotum and the structures on the anterior face of the front coxa.

In *Wormaldia* the black pigment on the side of the pronotum is in the shape of an "eyebrow" (Fig. 39, arrow *a*) and is not connected with the black band on the rear of the pronotum.   Also the anterior face of the front coxa carries a pale-coloured, thick, curved spine (Fig. 39, arrow *b*).

In *Chimarra marginata* the black pigment is in the form of an ovoid spot (Fig. 40, arrow *a*), and the front coxa has a long process surmounted by a black bristle (Fig. 40, arrow *b*).

In *Philopotamus montanus* the black pigment is in the form of a band which is continuous with the black band on the rear of the pronotum (Fig. 41, arrow *a*).   The front coxa has a rounded protuberance carrying a black bristle (Fig. 41, arrow *b*).

The reinstatement of *Wormaldia mediana* McLachlan brings the number of *Wormaldia* species in the British list to three, the other two being *W. subnigra* McLachlan and *W. occipitalis* (Pictet) (Kimmins 1953, 1965).   To date we have failed to find useful characters to separate the larvae of the three species.

Philopotamus montanus and *Wormaldia* larvae are common in the rapids of small fast-flowing streams.   Kimmins (1965) suggests on the basis of adult distribution that *W. occipitalis* is more widely distributed than either *W. mediana* or *W. subnigra*.   *Chimarra marginata* appears to extend into larger streams than the other species of Philopotamidae.

All the philopotamid larvae spin nets in the form of long tubular bags (Fig. 137) which they use to filter out small-sized food particles (p. 65).

POLYCENTROPODIDAE

Neureclipsis bimaculata

This species differs from all other polycentropodid larvae in having a pair of stout spines on the ventral side of the 9th abdominal segment (Fig. 42, arrows *b*; 43) and in the absence of bristles on the basal segment of the anal prolegs (Fig. 42, arrows *a*).   Additional distinguishing features for *Neureclipsis* are the straight line of spots on the posterior part of the frontoclypeus (Fig. 45) and the numerous small spines on the inside edge of the anal claw (Fig. 44).   These various characters are useful in 3rd to 5th instar larvae.   In smaller larvae the ventral spines on the 9th segment are longer and extend to the base of the anal prolegs.

Unlike most polycentropodid nets which are very variable in form, *Neureclipsis* nets are sufficiently distinctive to assist in species recognition. They are invariably trumpet-shaped with a narrow tail looping forward (Fig. 133).   *Neureclipsis* is localized in its geographical distribution in Britain and is usually found in lake outflow streams.

Genus CYRNUS

Cyrnus larvae always have four blunt teeth on the inside margin of the anal claw (Fig. 46). This is a reliable character even for early instar larvae and should be easily detectable with a binocular microscope using ×50 magnification.

C. trimaculatus is the most distinctive of the three species with dark bands of pigment on the dorsal side of the head (Fig. 47). In *C. flavidus* and *C. insolutus* the patterns are muted and the important difference between them is that in *flavidus* some of the dark posterior spots on the frontoclypeus fall within the central light area, whereas this is not the case with *C. insolutus* (Figs 48, 49). Other features of the head pattern are not sufficiently consistent to be used for identification.

C. trimaculatus is the commonest species, and is widely distributed in ponds, lakes and slow-flowing rivers. *C. flavidus* is localized and appears to be limited to still water. *C. insolutus* is rare in Britain and to date is known only from Blelham Tarn in the Lake District (Kimmins 1942, Edington 1964). However, adults and larvae have recently been collected in Ireland from Lough Derrygeeha in County Clare (O'Connor 1977).

Cyrnus larvae sometimes construct distinctive food-catching nets on aquatic plants (Fig. 134), but more often the nets are found under stones as irregular masses of threads (p. 62).

Genus POLYCENTROPUS

Later instar larvae of *Polycentropus* are distinguishable from the remaining genera in the key (*Plectrocnemia* and *Holocentropus*) by the shortness of the prothoracic tarsi relative to the tibiae (Fig. 50). Indeed the tarsal segment is so short in *Polycentropus* that there is a risk of mistaking it for part of the claw, especially if the leg is flexed. The distinction is less obvious with smaller larvae, and the segments are of equal length in the first instar. In *Polycentropus flavomaculatus*, for example, the ratio of tibia:tarsus length changes as follows: 5th instar 2·4:1, 4th instar 1·8:1, 3rd instar 1·5:1, 2nd instar 1·25:1, 1st instar 1:1.

Among the three *Polycentropus* species, *irroratus* is differentiated by having a head with a fairly uniform background colour against which the spots stand out very clearly (Fig. 52). In both *flavomaculatus* and *kingi* the head is distinctively banded and this is apparent even to the naked eye (Figs 53–55). Some difficulties may be encountered in separating these latter two species. *P. kingi* is best distinguished by having an obtuse-angled anal claw (Fig. 56) unlike *P. flavomaculatus* where the claw is right-angled (Fig. 57). In making this judgement it is important to view the side-face of the claw at right-angles, if necessary by examining it on a microscope slide.

In the material we have available there are also fairly subtle differences in head markings involving the relative position of spots and pigment areas on the frontoclypeus.   Each species has an arc of spots on the posterior part of the frontoclypeus, consisting typically of four large spots with two smaller and separate lateral ones.   In *P. flavomaculatus* (Figs 54, 55) these lateral spots are usually contained within the darkly-pigmented area, whereas in *P. kingi* (Fig. 53) they generally lie posterior to it.

P. flavomaculatus is the typical polycentropodid of the lower reaches of rivers; it is also common on stony lake shores.   *P. kingi* and *P. irroratus* are rarer and typically appear in small numbers in samples dominated by *P. flavomaculatus*.   The form of food-catching nets of *Polycentropus* is rarely apparent because they are usually built underneath stones and collapse into a mass of silk when the stone is overturned.

Genus PLECTROCNEMIA

Although three *Plectrocnemia* spp. are included in the British list, *Plectrocnemia brevis* McLachlan has appeared on only one occasion in 1903 (at Seaton, Devon) and it has not been possible to include it in the key.

Plectrocnemia larvae resemble *Holocentropus* larvae in having prothoracic tibiae and tarsi of approximately equal length, but differ from them in that *Plectrocnemia* has obtuse-angled anal claws (Fig. 58) whereas *Holocentropus* has right-angled ones (Fig. 59).

Fifth instar larvae (head width 1·85–2·70 mm) of *P. geniculata* and *P. conspersa* are most easily separated by the arrangements of bristles on the ventral side of the last (9th) abdominal segment.   In both species 4 pairs of primary bristles are present.   The distinction lies in the number and length of the secondary bristles.   In *P. geniculata* there are only about 6 pairs of these and most of them are short (Fig. 62).   In *P. conspersa* there are about 12 pairs and most of these are long (Fig. 60).

In 4th instar larvae (head width 1·30–1·75 mm) there are still 4 pairs of primary bristles in both species; but only 2–3 pairs of short secondary bristles in *P. geniculata* compared with 4–7 pairs of long ones in *P. conspersa*.

For the 4th and 5th instar larvae there is also a distinguishing feature on the labrum.   Both species have a thin line of dark pigment along the posterior border of the labrum.   In a median position in *P. conspersa* this line is expanded to form an elongate pigmented area (Fig. 61).   The pigmented area is not present in *P. geniculata* (Fig. 63).   To examine this feature it may be necessary to draw the labrum forward from underneath the plate behind it (the anteclypeus).

The head markings of *P. conspersa* are very variable; some individuals have a distinctly banded appearance (Fig. 65), others have a head which is a

fairly uniform dull-yellow (Fig. 66). The pigmentation pattern in
P. geniculata is much less variable (Fig. 64) and we have never found
individuals with the strongly contrasted pattern found in some *P. conspersa*
larvae.

P. conspersa rather than *P. flavomaculatus* is the common polycentropodid in the upper reaches of river systems. It also occurs in upland pools
and lakes. *P. geniculata* is more locally distributed but is also principally a
headwater and tributary species.

Plectrocnemia nets are often very conspicuous objects on the beds of small
streams. The form of the net varies with water depth and flow rate (p. 60,
Figs 127–131).

Genus HOLOCENTROPUS

Holocentropus larvae are considerably smaller, instar for instar, than
Plectrocnemia and differ in having right-angled rather than obtuse-angled
anal claws (Figs 58, 59). Head widths in 5th instar *Holocentropus* range
from 1·20 to 1·60 mm compared with 1·85–2·70 mm in *Plectrocnemia*.

There is usually no difficulty in separating the three *Holocentropus*
species from one another on the basis of head markings and head
shape. *H. dubius* has a superficial resemblance to *Cyrnus flavidus* but can
be distinguished by having pale areas inside *and* outside the frontoclypeus at
the point of constriction (Fig. 69); *C. flavidus* has only the outside marks
(Fig. 48). *Cyrnus* larvae should in any case have been intercepted at
couplet 17 of the key on the basis of their toothed anal claws.

Where *H. picicornis* and *H. dubius* live together in the same site their life
cycles may be staggered, with the result that throughout the winter
H. dubius larvae are the larger of the two (p. 79).

Holocentropus larvae occur in the still waters of lakes, ponds and
canals. *H. stagnalis* seems to be more local in its distribution than the other
two species. *Holocentropus* nets take the form of plate-like or funnel-
shaped structures attached to aquatic vegetation (p. 62, Fig. 132).

PSYCHOMYIIDAE
Psychomyia pusilla and *Metalype fragilis*

These two species are readily distinguishable from other psychomyiids by
the diagonal black thickening on the posterior-lateral margin of the
pronotum (Fig. 70, arrow). They can be separated from each other on the
form of the ventral head sclerites. In *Psychomyia pusilla* the anterior
paired sclerites (forming the mentum) are black and heavily ornamented,
with each plate as long as it is broad (Fig. 72). The corresponding plates in
Metalype fragilis are brown and smooth, lack ornamentation and each plate
is about half as long as it is broad (Fig. 73). The single plate behind the

mentum (i.e. the prementum) also differs in the two species; in *P. pusilla* it is in the form of a small regular triangle (Fig. 72), whereas in *M. fragilis* it is considerably expanded laterally (Fig. 73).   There are also differences in the number of spines on the anal claws.   In *P. pusilla* there are 5 or 6 (Fig. 74) and in *M. fragilis* 2 or 3 (Figs 75, 76).   These various characters allow the separation of the larvae in the 3rd, 4th and 5th (final) instars.

Psychomyia pusilla larvae grow slowly in winter (Fig. 149) so that when they occur at the same site as a faster-growing species, such as *Tinodes dives* (Fig. 147), there can be a marked difference in size between the two species in the early part of the year.

P. pusilla is common in large streams and rivers.   *M. fragilis* is rare and the few available records suggest that it is associated with calcareous streams and lakes.

Genus LYPE

Lype larvae differ from *Tinodes* larvae in having one (Fig. 78, arrow) rather than two vertical bars (Fig. 77, arrows) on the 1st coxopleurite.

The separation of *Lype reducta* and *Lype phaeopa* presents some difficulty.   In our material the band of pigment across the dorsal side of the head is darker in *L. reducta* and consequently divides the frontoclypeus into a posterior dark and an anterior light zone (Fig. 79).   No such clear division is apparent in *L. phaeopa* and in most specimens the frontoclypeus is virtually uniform in colour (Fig. 80).   In addition, the spots on the ventral surface of the head are usually more distinct in *L. reducta* (Fig. 81) than *L. phaeopa* (Fig. 82).   However these distinguishing features need to be confirmed by reared material from a wider range of localities.

Both *Lype* species construct galleries on submerged branches in streams, rivers, ponds and lakes.   The walls of the galleries consist of wood fragments and sand grains held together with silk.   Although there has been a tendency to regard *L. reducta* as the rarer of the two species (Hickin 1967) both species appear to be common in South Wales (Edington & Alderson 1973, Jenkins 1977).

Genus TINODES

Tinodes waeneri

Mature larvae of *T. waeneri* are easily separated from other *Tinodes* larvae by the distinctive markings on the head and pronotum, which are apparent even to the naked eye (Figs 84, 85).   These markings are clear in 5th instar larvae, sometimes apparent in 4th and 3rd but absent in 2nd and

1st. However all *T. waeneri* larvae whatever their size can be recognized by six microscopic teeth on the inside margin of the anal claw (Fig. 83). No other species of *Tinodes* has these teeth.

T. waeneri is widely distributed on stony lake shores and in large streams and rivers.

Tinodes unicolor, T. rostocki and T. dives

The remaining species of *Tinodes* can be grouped according to the pigmentation of the labrum. In *T. unicolor* the labrum is a uniform pale yellow colour (Fig. 86); in *T. rostocki* and *T. dives* it is a fairly even black or dark brown (Fig. 87), and in *T. pallidulus*, *T. maculicornis*, *T. assimilis* and *T. maclachlani* there is an irregular distribution of dark pigment with a concentration around the posterior-lateral points (Fig. 88). In examining the labrum for these features it is usually necessary to detach it from the head and to view it against a light background, otherwise the posterior-lateral points cannot be properly examined and the dark mandibles behind the labrum may make it difficult to discern its colour pattern. These features of the labrum are apparent in 4th and 5th instar larvae.

T. unicolor, although distinguishable by its pale labrum, has head markings (Fig. 90) which are otherwise similar to other *Tinodes* species (Figs 89, 95, 96). *T. unicolor* is particularly associated with calcareous streams, often where tufa is being deposited. It seems to grow slowly in winter and at this time of the year its larvae and galleries are noticeably smaller than those of fast-growing species such as *T. dives*.

The separation of *T. rostocki* and *T. dives* presents some difficulties. In newly preserved specimens the 2nd and 3rd coxopleurites are distinctly darker in *dives* (Fig. 92) than in *rostocki* (Fig. 91). This effect is produced by the thicker black horizontal bar in *dives* and the darker curved plate, ventral to it. There are also some features on the coxopleurite of the 1st leg which allow the separation of most specimens. The coxopleurite has a ventral notch into which the head of the coxa fits. Dorsal to this notch is a U- or V-shaped black thickening with two upwardly projecting arms. In *T. rostocki* the posterior arm is always long and sharply defined (Fig. 93, arrow) whereas in *T. dives* the posterior arm is short or, in darkly-pigmented individuals, terminates in an area of diffuse pigment (Fig. 94, arrow). In addition, the horizontal bar connecting the base of the arms is narrow and clearly defined in *rostocki*, but short and thick in *dives*. The overall effect is for the structure to appear as a U with unequal arms in *rostocki* and as a V in *dives*. To examine these features it may be necessary to separate the coxopleurite from the pronotum. This can be done most conveniently by keeping the coxopleurite attached to the foreleg.

In the uplands of South Wales *T. dives* occupies the moorland head waters and gives way to *T. rostocki* in the lower wooded valleys. This distribution would agree with Mosely's (1939) description of *T. dives* as an alpine and sub-alpine species.

Tinodes pallidulus

T. pallidulus is separable from other species with uneven pigmentation of the labrum by the prominent large pale spot in the posterior region of the frontoclypeus (Fig. 97). Occasionally, two lateral spots are present but these are always inconspicuous. By contrast, in *T. maculicornis*, *T. assimilis* and *T. maclachlani* the frontoclypeus has a line of three pale spots of more uniform size and colour (Figs 95, 96). Also in these three species the spots on the rest of the head are more conspicuous.

In Britain *T. pallidulus* has been recorded only from two small streams in Surrey (Kimmins 1949, Hickin 1950, 1953), but can no longer be found at these localities.

Tinodes maculicornis

Until recently in the British Isles this species was known only from a few Irish records of adults dating from the turn of the century. However, it has now been re-discovered in Ireland by O'Connor & Wise (1980), who have also discussed how the larvae can be distinguished from other psycho-myiids. *T. maculicornis* resembles *T. assimilis* and *T. maclachlani* in having a labrum with uneven pigmentation and a frontoclypeus with three similar pale spots in the posterior region. It differs from these two species in having no reddish pigment patch on the underside of the 2nd thoracic segment. In *T. assimilis* and *T. maclachlani* this patch (Fig. 98, arrow) can often be made more conspicuous by illuminating it from the side. We discovered that the patch fades in preservatives, such as Pampel's fluid, which contain acetic acid, and in these circumstances it cannot be used as a diagnostic feature. This is a strong argument for preserving psychomyiid larvae in alcohol.

The Irish records for *T. maculicornis* to date suggest that it is associated with the stony shores of calcareous lakes (O'Connor & Wise 1980).

Tinodes assimilis and T. maclachlani

As is described in the key, *T. assimilis* can be distinguished from *T. maclachlani* using the pigmentation patterns on the prolegs and 1st coxopleurite (Figs 99–102). When comparing the colour of the trochantin with the rest of the coxopleurite it is advisable to remove the head to prevent it from forming a coloured background behind the semi-transparent trochantin.

Vertical or near-vertical rock faces over which thin films of water are flowing, the so-called 'hygropetric habitat' (Vaillant 1953, 1954, Hickin 1967) are typical sites for both *T. assimilis* and *T. maclachlani.* In these situations a large proportion of the rock face may be covered with larval galleries. In lowland areas *T. maclachlani* may extend into more typical small stream habitats. Possibly this is related to the absence of *T. dives* from small lowland streams (p. 73).

Although in areas of easily weathered rock strata psychomyiid larvae are often very abundant (Plate 1b) they are frequently overlooked; possibly as a result of the superficial resemblance of their galleries to the silt tubes of chironomids.

HYDROPSYCHIDAE

Twelve species of hydropsychids could be considered to qualify for inclusion in the British list. Two of these, *Hydropsyche exocellata* Dufour and *Hydropsyche guttata* Pictet, were found in the lower reaches of the River Thames in the last century but have since disappeared, presumably as a result of pollution. There have been no records for *H. exocellata* since 1901 and for *H. guttata* since 1915 (Badcock 1976) and they may now be extinct in Britain. In the absence of larval material it has not been possible to include them in the key.

Neither have we been able to examine British material of *Hydropsyche saxonica* McLachlan, a species which has evidently disappeared from its only known locality near Oxford (Badcock 1976). However in this instance some incomplete descriptions are available, based partly on continental material (Lepneva 1970, Sedlák 1971, Badcock 1977) and we have been able to suggest some features to distinguish this species from *Hydropsyche fulvipes* (Curtis) which it most nearly resembles (p. 58).

The claim (Malicky 1977) that *Hydropsyche bulgaromanorum* Malicky occurs (or has occurred) in Britain is so far based on two adults of possibly doubtful provenance discovered in continental museum collections. This claim needs to be investigated further. The larvae of this species have not been described.

This leaves eight species which undoubtedly still occur in Britain and the key is designed to allow their separation.

Cheumatopsyche lepida

This species differs from all other hydropsychid larvae in having a dense covering of long bristles on the dorsal and anterior part of the pronotum and on the dorsal surface of the head capsule (Fig. 103). In addition the posterior prosternites (a pair of plates on the ventral side of the 1st thoracic segment) are very much smaller in *Cheumatopsyche* (Fig. 109) than in the various *Hydropsyche* species (Fig. 110). In *Diplectrona felix* they are absent altogether. *C. lepida* is by far the smallest of the British hydropsychids and final instar larvae, when extended, measure about 1 cm in length. This value is comfortably exceeded by all other species at the same stage. *C. lepida* is relatively uncommon and usually occurs in the lower reaches of rivers.

Diplectrona felix

D. felix can be easily distinguished from other hydropsychids by the uniformly brown dorsal surface of the head (Fig. 105). The other species all have yellow marks on the head (Figs 121–126) although these are less obvious in early instars. In addition, *D. felix* is characterized by the shape of the frontoclypeus, which is constricted at about the level of the eyes (Fig. 105) and not smooth in outline as it is in the other species (Figs 121–126). The posterior prosternites are absent in *D. felix* and the prothoracic trochantin has a single (Fig. 106) rather than a double point (Figs 103, 104).

D. felix is widespread in Britain although commonest in the north and west (Badcock 1976). It is restricted to small streams and springs which remain cool in summer (p. 70).

Hydropsyche siltalai

This is the most easily distinguished of the *Hydropsyche* larvae because of the absence of gills on the 7th abdominal segment (Fig. 107). In all other *Hydropsyche* species gills are present on this segment (Fig. 108). When identifying the 7th segment it is best to count backwards down the dorsal side of the animal, because the segments may be misleadingly compressed ventrally by the curvature of the body. Abdominal gills are present in *Hydropsyche* larvae from the 2nd instar onwards so that this character can be used for all but the smallest larvae (Table 1, p. 75, gives the head capsule widths for various instars).

H. siltalai is the most widespread and abundant of the British hydropsychids (Badcock 1976, Crichton et al. 1978). It lives in fast-flowing rivers and streams, often in company with *H. pellucidula* (p. 72). Where these two species occur together there is usually a marked size difference between them in the winter months. *H. pellucidula* grows rapidly in autumn and usually passes the winter in the 5th instar, whereas *H. siltalai* typically reaches only the 3rd instar by this time (p. 79, Figs 144, 145).

Hydropsyche contubernalis

Larvae of *H. contubernalis* can be distinguished from other *Hydropsyche* species in having posterior prosternites which are uniformly pale (Fig. 111), rather than dark (Fig. 112) or bicoloured (Figs 113–115). The species is also recognizable by the two distinctive yellow patches on the frontoclypeus (Fig. 121). Somewhat similar patches are evident in *H. siltalai* (Fig. 122) but this latter species should have keyed out earlier. *H. contubernalis* is usually found in the lower reaches of large rivers (Badcock 1976).

Hydropsyche angustipennis, H. pellucidula, H. fulvipes and H. instabilis

Four sets of characters are useful in separating these remaining species, and rather than make an arbitrary selection to produce a dichotomous key, we have presented the alternatives in tabular form (p. 44).

Posterior prosternites

On the basis of this character *H. angustipennis* differs from the other three species in having both the lateral and medial regions of the prosternites darkened (Fig. 112). Sometimes the medial regions are slightly darker than the lateral ones, but in all cases the two sections together appear as a dark narrow strip. In the other three species the lateral regions of the prosternites are invariably pale (Figs 113–115).

H. fulvipes differs from *H. pellucidula* and *H. instabilis* in having the median parts of the prosternites roughly triangular (Fig. 114) rather than rectangular (Figs 113, 115).

Mentum

This plate, situated anteriorly on the underside of the head (Fig. 116), varies in form in the four species. In *H. pellucidula* (Fig. 117) and *H. angustipennis* (Fig. 118) the median channel is straight-sided, whereas in *H. instabilis* (Fig. 119) and *H. fulvipes* (Fig. 120) it is shaped like an inverted key-hole. Although both have a straight-sided median channel, the mentum of *H. pellucidula* (Fig. 117) differs from that of *H. angustipennis* (Fig. 118) in having squarer lateral margins. It may be necessary to remove the mentum and mount it on a slide to see these features properly. Badcock (1955) has also drawn attention to differences in the colour of the mentum. In *H. instabilis* and *H. fulvipes* it is usually darker centrally than at the margins, whereas in *H. pellucidula* and *H. angustipennis* the margins are darker than the centre. However these colour characters are less satisfactory for early instar or newly moulted larvae.

Frontoclypeus

The four species can also be separated using the shape and the markings of the frontoclypeus. In *H. pellucidula* (Fig. 126) and *H. angustipennis* (Fig. 125) the frontoclypeus is V-shaped in outline and sharply pointed posteriorly. By contrast the frontoclypeus in *H. fulvipes* (Fig. 123) and *H. instabilis* (Fig. 124) is rounded posteriorly and roughly U-shaped in outline.

The surface of the frontoclypeus is noticeably rougher in texture in *angustipennis* than in the other three species.

There are potentially four pale marks on the dorsal surface of the frontoclypeus; these comprise single anterior and posterior marks and paired lateral ones (e.g. Fig. 124). Although the pattern of marks varies somewhat within each species, once an appreciation has been made of the range of variation at a particular locality, the routine separation of species in large samples can often be made principally on the basis of these marks.

In *H. angustipennis* (Fig. 125) only the two lateral marks are obvious, the posterior mark is indistinct and the anterior mark usually absent. *H. pellucidula* (Fig. 126) has obvious lateral and posterior marks and usually a distinguishable anterior one. The posterior mark takes the form of a Y or a single longitudinal streak. In *H. instabilis* (Fig. 124) the posterior mark takes the form of a U or V (not a Y or longitudinal bar as in *H. pellucidula*); the lateral marks are also clear, but the anterior mark may be absent. *H. fulvipes* (Fig. 123) has a very characteristic pattern in that the lateral marks are fused with the posterior mark to form an extended irregular V-shape. The tip of the V is usually slightly darker than the rest. The large anterior mark is commonly very nearly fused with the laterals.

H. saxonica appears to have frontoclypeal markings resembling those of *H. fulvipes* but a V-shaped frontoclypeus like that seen in *H. angustipennis* and *H. pellucidula* (Lepneva 1970, Sedlák 1971, Badcock 1977).

H. pellucidula is widely distributed and abundant in large streams and rivers, and frequently occurs in mixed populations with *H. siltalai*. *H. instabilis* is found in medium sized fast-flowing streams, usually well upstream from *H. pellucidula* but often overlapping with *H. siltalai* (Fig. 138). *H. angustipennis* has a markedly southern and midland distribution in Britain (Badcock 1976, Crichton et al. 1978) and can be found in rivers and streams of all sizes. Amongst the hydropsychid species it appears to be the most tolerant of high temperatures and organic pollution, and the few existing records for Scotland and Northern England are from the warm outflows of ponds and lakes. *H. fulvipes* is very local in distribution and is known from a few small streams in the north and west of Britain (Hildrew & Morgan 1974, Badcock 1975).

The nets of hydropsychid larvae are often a striking feature of streams and rivers, particularly where bed rock rapids covered with moss carpets have been colonized (Plate 1a).

ECNOMIDAE

Although our only British species *Ecnomus tenellus* (Rambur) has previously been included in the family Psychomyiidae, *Ecnomus* larvae are quite unlike psychomyiid larvae in having dorsal plates on all three thoracic segments, a lateral fringe of bristles on the abdomen and a pointed rather than a leaf-like trochantin (Fig. 23, compared with a typical psychomyiid larva in Fig. 17). These and other features led Lepneva (1956, 1970) to place *Ecnomus* in a separate family, an arrangement we have followed here.

Ecnomus larvae are found in ponds, canals, lakes and large rivers. Their exact mode of life has still not been elucidated (p. 66).

FEEDING BIOLOGY

There is a close relationship between the feeding techniques of the larvae and their constructional activities. For instance, the Psychomyiidae build fixed galleries on the surfaces of stones or rotting wood and scrape food from the substratum at the gallery mouth. Larvae of the Philopotamidae, Hydropsychidae and Polycentropodidae all spin nets, but the form of the nets and the situations in which they are operated vary greatly from one family to another. Philopotamid nets have fine meshes and filter very small particles from a limited volume of water. Hydropsychid nets are coarser meshed and trap proportionally larger food items from a large volume of water. Polycentropodid nets are different again and are used as traps or snares to catch live prey from slowly flowing or still waters.

Rhyacophilid larvae make no larval construction of any kind and live by actively foraging for prey, generally in fast-flowing parts of streams.

The feeding habits of the different groups will now be examined in detail.

POLYCENTROPODIDAE

The nets spun by polycentropodid larvae consist basically of a silken tube, in which the larva rests, extended at each end into two, often asymmetric, catching surfaces (Fig. 128). The nets are never built in fast-flowing waters and therefore differ from the filter feeding devices used by the Philopotamidae and Hydropsychidae. Polycentropodid nets are generally operated as snares which capture live prey, whether it is passively drifting, actively swimming or crawling over the substratum. The mesh of the nets is generally coarser and more irregular than in the other families.

Townsend & Hildrew (1979) have shown that the nets constructed by *Plectrocnemia conspersa* vary in form according to flow rate and water depth. In flow-rates between 4·5 and 20 cm s^{-1} (the upper limit for this species) the two catching funnels are orientated into the current as if to catch drifting prey (Figs 127, 128). In slower-flowing water, net form is related to water depth. In water less than about 5 cm deep, or where a projection such as a twig comes near the surface, many of the net threads of the catching funnels are attached to the surface film (Fig. 129). In deeper water the nets are often in the form of extensive, flat areas of meshwork (up to 15 cm across) attached to stones and leaves on the stream bed (Figs 130, 131). Larvae with surface nets usually catch significantly more terrestrial prey and emerging chironomids, although after heavy rain these items are taken by nets of all types.

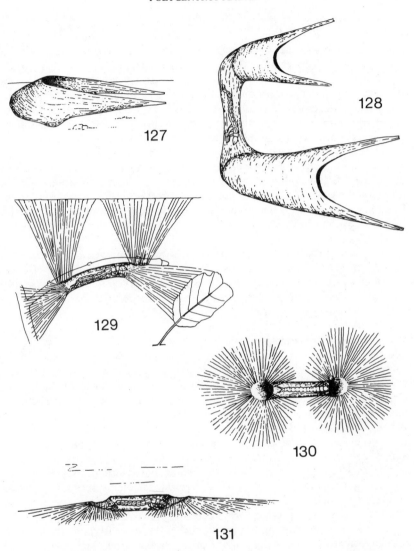

Figs. 127–131. Types of nets constructed by *Plectrocnemia conspersa* larvae: 127, 128: catching nets constructed at flow rates between 4·5 and 20 cm s⁻¹ (side and plan views); 129: net constructed in shallow water at slow flow rates (side view); 130, 131: net constructed in deep water at slow flow rates (plan and side views).

More is known about the net form of *Plectrocnemia conspersa* than that of *Polycentropus flavomaculatus*, although the latter is one of our most abundant caddis species.   The nets of *P. conspersa* are more often built in exposed and superficial situations than those of *Polycentropus*. *Polycentropus* larvae are, instar for instar, much smaller than *Plectrocnemia*, perhaps enabling them to use smaller crevices for net-spinning.   Although Wesenberg-Lund (1911) described the nets of *P. flavomaculatus* as being shaped like "swallows' nests", they are more usually encountered as shapeless masses of silk which collapse when the supporting stone has been overturned.

The net of *Neureclipsis bimaculata* is very distinctive and takes the form of a long, trumpet-shaped catching funnel (up to 20 cm long) with a narrower living-tube turned to point back upstream (Fig. 133) (Alm 1926, Brickenstein 1955).   The species feeds on drifting animals and is usually found in lake outflows where it catches planktonic organisms carried by the current.

Holocentropus nets are to be found attached to aquatic vegetation and consist of sheet-like or funnel-shaped structures with tubular retreats (Wesenberg-Lund 1911, Alm 1926) (Fig. 132).   *Cyrnus* nets are usually sited under stones, although *Cyrnus flavidus* is recorded as building conical nets on the leaves of water plants (Wesenberg-Lund 1911) (Fig. 134).

The British Polycentropodidae are exclusively predatory (Percival & Whitehead 1929, Badcock 1949, Jones 1949, 1950, Tachet 1965, 1971b, Hildrew & Townsend 1976, Townsend & Hildrew 1978).   The exact composition of the diet is variable from place to place according to the prey available.   The still-water forms take a variety of rotifers, Cladocera, Copepoda and Ostracoda and, in addition, larger larvae take Oligochaeta and chironomid larvae (Higler 1978).   Stream-dwelling polycentropodids take mainly larvae of Chironomidae, Ephemeroptera and Plecoptera and, in the earlier instars, benthic Crustacea.   *Plectrocnemia conspersa* takes appreciable quantities of terrestrial prey.

The most complete description of feeding behaviour is that of Tachet (1971a, b, 1977) for *Plectrocnemia conspersa*.   He describes seven phases of predatory behaviour, beginning with the alerting of the larva to the presence of prey, through prey capture, to the final grooming and toilet.   The major stimulus to prey capture is the generation of vibrations in the net threads by the struggling of prey animals after they have become entangled in the mesh.   It was found that vibrations were reduced in amplitude slightly during transmission across the net, but the frequency was unchanged.   Complete sequences of predatory behaviour were stimulated experimentally by vibrations in the range 0·28–7·50 Hz.   The net of *P. conspersa* therefore seems to be used rather like that of many

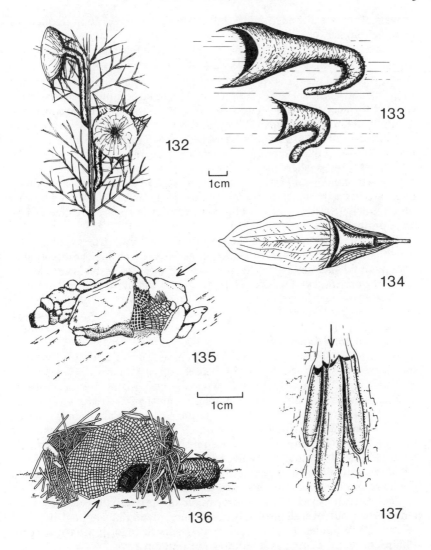

Figs 132–137.   Net types: 132 – *Holocentropus dubius* (after Wesenberg-Lund 1911); 133 – *Neureclipsis bimaculata*; 134 – *Cyrnus flavidus* on a leaf of *Potamogeton lucens* (after Wesenberg-Lund 1911); 135 – *Hydropsyche angustipennis* net supported by stones (after Sattler 1958); 136 – *Hydropsyche angustipennis* net supported by plant fragments (after Lepneva 1970); 137 – *Philopotamus montanus*.

terrestrial spiders although, in the latter, the relevant vibration frequencies are much higher.

HYDROPSYCHIDAE

Hydropsychid nets are typically constructed in rapidly flowing water, and in spring and summer they are often to be seen in large numbers on the moss-covered surfaces of stones (Plate 1a). In these situations the net consists of a simple tubular retreat, open at both ends, spun between the moss stems and extended anteriorly into an obvious arched canopy with a rear filtration area and a wide mouth. Nets are also constructed in crevices between and underneath stones where pieces of gravel or plant material are often used to support the canopy and retreat tube (Figs 135, 136). The nets are usually orientated at right angles to the water current but in very fast flows may be set obliquely (Sattler 1958). The flow of water is apparently detected by setae on the dorsal surface of the head (Kaiser 1965).

The central filtering area of the net has a very regular rectangular mesh which, although it varies from species to species, is much coarser than that of philopotamid larvae. The average mesh size for 5th instar larvae of *Hydropsyche siltalai* and *H. instabilis* is about 300×170 µm and 315×145 µm respectively (Hildrew & Edington 1979). The mesh size of *H. pellucidula* is larger (368×240 µm) and that of *H. angustipennis* smaller (205×112 µm) whilst *Diplectrona felix* has a somewhat squarer mesh (260×200 µm) (Kaiser 1965).

It is well established that the average mesh size of hydropsychid nets increases with instar (Sattler 1963, Kaiser 1965, Williams & Hynes 1973, Wallace 1975, Wallace, Webster & Woodall 1977, Malas & Wallace 1977, Wallace & Merritt 1980). For example, a typical mesh size for a 2nd instar *Hydropsyche* larva is only about 80×50 µm. There is also some variation of mesh size within a single net. Malas & Wallace (1977) found that the smallest meshes of two North American hydropsychid nets were in that part closest to the substratum where the water velocity would be reduced. In all nets the mesh of the outer area of the filtering canopy is quite irregular and the larva frequently allows this part to become blocked by debris.

The British species of Hydropsychidae are usually described as omnivorous but overall probably take more plant than animal material (Percival & Whitehead 1929, Slack 1936, Badcock 1949, Jones 1949, 1950, Philipson 1953a, Scott 1958, Hildrew & Edington 1979).

The feeding behaviour of *Hydropsyche siltalai* in its net has been described by Philipson (1953a). The larva holds itself in position by the anal appendages and meso- and metathoracic legs, while the prothoracic legs are held close to the undersurface of the head which is then moved rapidly from side to side, over the central area of the net. Any particles are rapidly seized using the mandibles and prothoracic legs. Some selection is exercised and inedible mineral particles are ejected from the net mouth into the current or incorporated into the net structure with silk strands.

There is some evidence that *Hydropsyche* larvae sometimes feed independently of the net (Krawany 1930, Badcock 1949, Jones 1950, Schumacher 1970, Williams & Hynes 1973). Schumacher (1970) considers that the larvae simply browse periphyton off the stones and that nets are used as artificial substrata to feed from only in particular circumstances. We have never observed this mode of feeding either in the laboratory or in the field but the point does require clarification.

PHILOPOTAMIDAE

Larvae of this family spin nets in the form of long, tubular bags with small mouths (Fig. 137). They are found most frequently in small upland streams where the water drains through piles of boulders. If a boulder is removed they may be seen hanging attached at the anterior end, glistening and distended with water. Nets are also occasionally found on exposed vertical rock faces.

Some older illustrations of philopotamid nets (e.g. by Ruttner 1963) show them with a large terminal hole. Although larvae frequently leave the net at this point if disturbed, no microscopical evidence for a permanent hole could be found. Indian ink suspensions introduced at the mouth of a *Philopotamus montanus* net took some minutes to disperse through the walls and did not issue through a terminal hole.

The mesh size of philopotamid nets proves to be very much smaller than was originally thought. Wallace & Malas (1976) found that the North American species *Dolophilodes distinctus* had meshes ranging from $0 \cdot 2 \times 2 \cdot 5$ μm in 2nd instar larvae up to $1 \cdot 75 \times 5 \cdot 5$ μm in 5th instar larvae. We found that nets of 5th instar larvae of *Philopotamus montanus* had a similar structure. The wall of the bag consists of a fine rectangular framework with longitudinal strands 10–13 μm apart and minor transverse strands 25–70 μm apart. There are, in addition, finer transverse strands less than 1 μm apart (Plate 2). Each strand is made up of a double filament.

Philopotamid larvae evidently filter very small particles indeed. The most extensive data on their diet are those of Wallace, Webster & Woodall (1977) and Malas & Wallace (1977). They show that the average size of detritus particles in the guts of *Dolophilodes distinctus* was 5 μm^2 with some less than 1 μm^2. Information on the British species is rather limited although there is every indication that detritus and diatoms are the main dietary constituents. Philipson (1953b) and Jones (1949) found these items in the guts of *Wormaldia subnigra* and *Philopotamus montanus* respectively.   Our own observations showed that *P. montanus* guts were filled with a mass of gritty detritus and diatoms with a very few small fragments of higher plant tissue.

The uniformly small size of particles in the guts of philopotamid larvae is consistent with the fine mesh of their nets.   It seems that the absence of any larger particles in the diet is due, firstly, to the overall shape of the net and, secondly, to the behaviour of the larva.   The net mouth is very restricted and, because of the flow patterns created, we found it quite difficult to introduce larger particles into the net using a pipette.   When we did succeed in introducing fragments of moss or small live animals such as chironomid larvae, the caddis always vigorously ejected them from the net mouth.   Normally, fine food particles which collect on the inner wall are gathered by downward sweeping movements of the brush-like labrum (Philipson 1953b).

ECNOMIDAE

Information is lacking on the feeding behaviour of the only British species, *Ecnomus tenellus*.   When *Ecnomus* was classed as a psychomyiid it was usually tacitly assumed that it fed like other psychomyiids by scraping encrusting algae from stones.   However, it now seems possible that it is a net-spinner and this would be consistent with its occurrence in beds of water plants (Jenkins 1977, Higler 1978).   More information is obviously needed on the feeding habits of this species.

PSYCHOMYIIDAE

These gallery-building caddis larvae are particularly characteristic of streams running over easily weathered rocks, and lakes with stony substrata.   Psychomyiid galleries are fixed, tunnel-like, structures (Plate 1b) and thus contrast with both the nets and transportable cases of other caddis larvae.   They have been described by Berg (1938), Danecker (1961), Hickin (1967) and Alderson (1969).   In cross-section the gallery walls form an arch with a sufficiently large internal diameter to allow the larva within to turn round on itself.   The gallery length varies according to species from two to seven times the larval length.

The galleries are constructed from fragments of mineral or other materials held together by silk.   In *Tinodes waeneri*, which uses mineral particles, Jones (1976a) has shown that there is some selection of particle size.   Fourth instar larvae were found to choose particles of 0·2 and 0·5 mm diameter whilst 5th instars chose those of 1 mm.   This selection is probably related to the mandibular gape of the larvae. Alderson (1969) found that sand grains were the most frequently used material in the field, especially for those species inhabiting streams and rivers. In thin water films running over rocks, however, he found that the galleries of *Tinodes dives, T. maclachlani, T. assimilis* and *T. unicolor* consisted largely of faecal pellets. If there is a thick algal mat on the substratum, pieces may be bitten off and incorporated into the gallery. The two species of *Lype* are distinctive in that they build their galleries on submerged branches and use fragments of woody material. These may be derived from faecal pellets or directly from the substratum. The galleries are usually broader at the anterior end than the posterior.

Descriptions of feeding of psychomyiid larvae have been given by Danecker (1961), Jones (1976b) and, most extensively, by Alderson (1969). The larva partially emerges from the front of the gallery and grazes material from the substratum. In this position it can quickly withdraw if disturbed since the anal hooks maintain a firm grip on the floor of the gallery. The larva scrapes at the substratum with its mandibles, which in consequence are often found to be worn down at the tip. The labrum is held over the mandibles while the maxillae extend below, thus forming a cavity in which food is collected. The fine hairs on the maxillae and on the lower surface of the mandibles probably serve to prevent the loss of small particles. The tip of the right mandible scrapes food along a groove in the left mandible and it is conveyed from here to the mouth. When the food supply is exhausted around the gallery mouth, the larva demolishes the hind end of the gallery and extends it at the front. The galleries thus gradually change position as feeding progresses.

The larvae in this family fall into two groups based on their diet. *Lype* species feed on wood and the others mainly on algae, although animal remains have been recorded from the gut of *Tinodes waeneri* (Dunn 1954). Since the larvae feed by scraping surfaces, they inevitably ingest a good deal of inorganic matter.

Alderson (1969) has provided evidence from his studies in South Wales that some psychomyiid species are associated with particular algal communities. For example, *Tinodes unicolor* typically occurs in highly calcareous streams (calcium concentration > 60 mg l^{-1}) and feeds on the blue-green alga *Phormidium incrustatum*. This alga is to be found embedded in calcite incrustations and is involved in their deposition (Fritsch 1950). The larvae appear to gain access to the algal filaments by using an acid secretion which dissolves the surrounding calcite.

By contrast *Psychomyia pusilla* is particularly associated with sites where the spring diatom community is well-developed. This community includes species such as *Cymbella, Gomphonema, Navicula* and *Achnanthes*. The acceleration of growth rate of *Psychomyia* in April and May takes place when the larvae are feeding on the spring bloom of diatoms.

RHYACOPHILIDAE

Rhyacophila larvae neither spin nets nor build fixed galleries but are completely free-living. They appear to be actively foraging predators (Siltala 1907, Percival & Whitehead 1929, Slack 1936, Nielsen 1942, Badcock 1949, Jones 1949, Scott 1958). Major sources of prey are chironomid larvae and larvae of *Baetis* and *Simulium*. Diet varies, however, with the availability of prey. We have found that small *Hydropsyche* larvae are quite frequently taken and Fox (1978) showed that *Rhyacophila* would eat eggs of the bullhead (*Cottus gobio*). A fairly large proportion of individuals, especially the smaller instars, may be found with plant material in the gut. This could represent the remains of the gut contents of herbivorous prey animals (Nielsen 1942) but it seems more likely that the larvae sometimes actively feed on the algae and moss on stones.

HABITAT DISTRIBUTION

The distribution of the species can be considered at a number of different levels.   Firstly, they sometimes show distinctive geographic patterns within the British Isles and, where possible, we have mentioned such cases in the taxonomic section.   However, we feel that distribution maps, for all but the commonest species, would be more misleading than helpful at this stage.   Secondly, patterns of distribution along river systems are of interest and there is now a good deal of information on this aspect.   Thirdly, the micro-distribution patterns of larvae on the stream or river bed have received much attention.   Consequently it is these last two aspects of species distribution which are dealt with in particular here.

In British rivers there are well-marked downstream sequences of species in the families Hydropsychidae, Polycentropodidae and Psychomyiidae (Figs 138, 139).   These distribution patterns seem to be linked mainly with physical factors.   Within each family there would seem to be an adaptive radiation of species in relation to the various factor gradients down the length of watercourses.

At the microhabitat level, the distribution patterns of species can be related to variations in such factors as water velocity, substratum and food supply.

POLYCENTROPODIDAE

Some polycentropodid larvae, including *Cyrnus flavidus, C. insolutus, Holocentropus stagnalis* and *H. dubius,* appear to be restricted in Britain to still water.   *Neureclipsis bimaculata* is known only from running water, and the remaining species are found in both types of habitats.

In rivers, there is a clear sequential pattern of species, with *Plectrocnemia conspersa* or *P. geniculata* being normally found in small headwater streams and replaced downstream by *Polycentropus flavomaculatus* (Edington 1968, Edington & Hildrew 1973).   *Cyrnus trimaculatus* usually appears in the lower reaches of larger rivers.   Figure 139 shows a typical polycentro-podid distribution pattern from the River Usk in South Wales. This pattern apparently reflects physiological differences between the species, since Philipson & Moorhouse (1976) have shown that *Polycentropus flavomaculatus* is more tolerant than *Plectrocnemia conspersa* of the high temperatures and decreased oxygen concentrations, which characterize the lower reaches of rivers.

The microdistribution of polycentropodid larvae is related primarily to water velocity. Edington (1965, 1968) found that *Plectrocnemia conspersa* and *Polycentropus flavomaculatus* were most common in stream pools, in marked contrast with hydropsychid and philopotamid species, which were characteristic of rapids. This commitment to slow flow-rates is reflected in the mechanical properties of the net. For example, nets of *Plectrocnemia conspersa* disintegrate when subjected to velocities in excess of 20 cm s^{-1}. There are also major differences in respiratory physiology between polycentropodid and hydropsychid larvae. Philipson (1954) found, for instance, that *Polycentropus flavomaculatus* could utilize oxygen at relatively low concentrations, even in still water. *Hydropsyche siltalai*, on the other hand, needed both high concentrations of oxygen and flowing water to survive.

Even within the tolerable range of water velocity, up to about 20 cm s^{-1}, the distribution of *Plectrocnemia conspersa* larvae is not uniform. They tend to aggregate in parts of the stream bed where benthic prey density is highest (Hildrew & Townsend 1976), and in these favourable areas larvae may fight over net-spinning sites. In a laboratory stream, net-holders were observed to defend their territories from intruding larvae, with both individuals rearing up "face-to-face" and striking at each other with mandibles open. The larger of the two larvae normally won possession of the net, usually without obvious injury to either contestant (Hildrew & Townsend 1980).

HYDROPSYCHIDAE

In the Hydropsychidae the typical order of first appearance from source to mouth in sizeable unpolluted rivers is: *Diplectrona felix*; *Hydropsyche instabilis*; *Hydropsyche siltalai*; *Hydropsyche pellucidula*; *Hydropsyche contubernalis* and/or *Cheumatopsyche lepida* (Mackereth 1960, Edington 1968, Edington & Hildrew 1973, Badcock 1975, 1976, Boon 1979, Hildrew & Edington 1979). Figure 138 illustrates this sequence in the River Usk. We have found that *D. felix*, *H. instabilis* and *H. pellucidula* exhibit differences in their respiratory rate/temperature relationships which suggest that they are adapted to progressively higher summer temperatures. In the River Usk system, *D. felix* is characteristic of small streams with summer maxima up to 15 °C and small daily ranges. Further downstream, *H. instabilis* stations have higher summer maxima and larger daily ranges. In the main river, the *H. pellucidula* stations also have high maxima but much-reduced daily ranges. As might be expected, there are some departures from this general pattern. For example in headstreams which run from open moorland into wooded gorges, and where summer

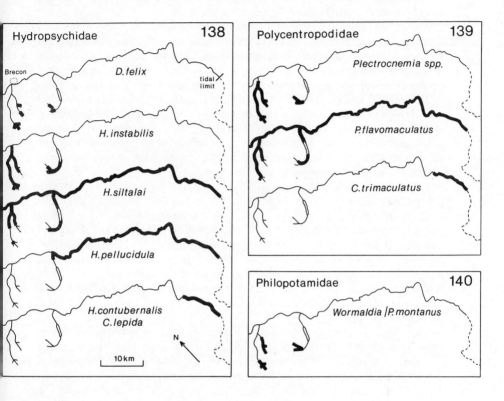

Figs 138–140.   Distribution of net-spinning caddis larvae in the main river and selected side tributaries in the River Usk system in South Wales.

temperatures decrease rather than increase downstream, *Hydropsyche instabilis* occurs upstream of *Diplectrona felix*.

Before the pollution of many large rivers, *H. exocellata* and *H. guttata* may have represented two further elements in the downstream sequence.   Both were known as adults from the lower reaches of the River Thames at the beginning of the century and Décamps (1968) has shown that on the Garonne the sequence does indeed conclude with these two species.

The other common British hydropsychid, *H. angustipennis*, seems to fall outside this general pattern.   It is sometimes found in the lower reaches of large rivers but also occurs in small streams, particularly the outflows of ponds and lakes.   This distribution may be related to its known tolerance of high temperatures, low oxygen concentrations and low water velocities (Ambühl 1959, Philipson & Moorhouse 1974).

In terms of microdistribution, hydropsychid larvae in Britain can generally be regarded as fast-flow specialists and as such are complementary both in distribution and physiological attributes to the pool-living polycentropodids (Philipson 1954, 1969, Edington 1965, 1968).   Recently however it has become apparent that, even within the Hydropsychidae, different water-velocity preferences occur.   In particular, *Hydropsyche pellucidula* has been shown, both in the field and the laboratory, to be more tolerant of slow flow-rates.   This may be an important factor in facilitating its coexistence with *H. siltalai* (Philipson & Moorhouse 1974, Boon 1978a, Hildrew & Edington 1979).

As in the Polycentropodidae, there is evidence that antagonistic behaviour may be important in determining microdistribution.   Johnstone (1964) first demonstrated that hydropsychid larvae could stridulate.   The sound is produced by the larva rubbing a scraper on the front femur (Plate 3) across a file on the underside of the head (Plate 4a, b).   The scraper takes the form of a protuberance bearing ridges of cuticle and the file is an area of cuticle with a number of wave-like folds on it.

Jansson & Vuoristo (1979) have recently provided experimental evidence that stridulation is used by larvae occupying nets as a means of repelling intruders, and they found that defenders which failed to stridulate were more likely to be evicted.   The regular spacing of nets in places where they are abundant (Plate 1a) certainly points to the existence of some kind of territorial or spacing mechanism.   Also Elliott (1968) found that *H. siltalai* larvae were particularly common drifting downstream in spring when rapid larval growth might be expected to increase competition for space.

There remains some doubt as to the most significant frequency in the sounds emitted by hydropsychid larvae.   Jansson & Vuoristo's analysis suggested that most of the energy lay below a frequency of 4 kHz. However, Silver (1980), using high-frequency equipment, reported strong

PLATE 1a.   Nets of *Hydropsyche instabilis* constructed on moss-covered bed rock.

PLATE 1b.   Larval galleries of *Tinodes rostocki*.

PLATE 2a.   Part of the net of *Philopotamus montanus* at low magnification.
(Scale line = 40 μm)

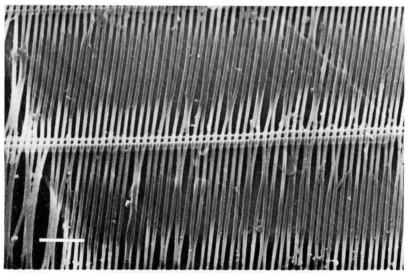

PLATE 2b.   Part of the net of *Philopotamus montanus* at high magnification.
(Scale line = 4 μm) (SEM photographs by D. Windsor).

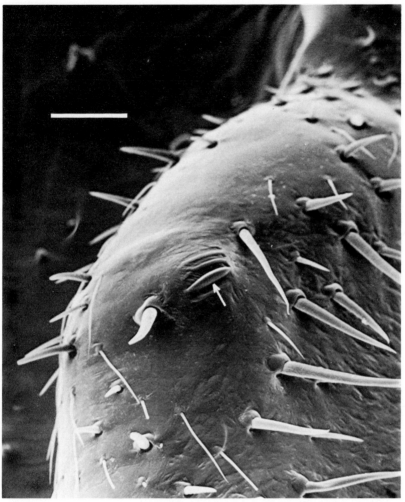

PLATE 3.   Stridulatory apparatus in *Hydropsyche siltalai*: scraper (arrow) on prothoracic femur. (Scale line = 100 μm) (SEM photograph by S. C. Silver).

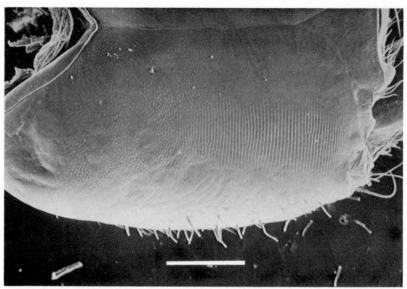

PLATE 4a.   Stridulatory apparatus in *Hydropsyche siltalai*. General view of file on ventral surface of head. (Scale line = 250 μm).

PLATE 4b.   Stridulatory apparatus in *Hydropsyche siltalai*. Enlarged view of file. (Scale line = 20 μm) (SEM photographs by S. C. Silver).

ultrasonic components up to 90 kHz.   She makes the interesting suggestion that such high frequencies might make possible the clear detection of oscillatory movements in the water at a range up to 2 cm, leaving the animals deaf to the background noise in a fast-flowing and turbulent stream.   As yet, however, there is no clear evidence of whether the high or low frequency components of the sound predominate, or of how they are detected by other individuals.

PHILOPOTAMIDAE

Philopotamus montanus and *Wormaldia* spp. occur typically in the rapids of headwaters and tributaries (Fig. 140) (Edington 1965, 1968).   Philipson (1953b) has shown in the laboratory that larvae of *W. subnigra* require high water velocities for net-spinning.

The rather sparse distribution records available for *Chimarra marginata* suggest that it extends into larger rivers than the other philopotamids.

ECNOMIDAE

The larvae of *Ecnomus tenellus* have been collected from the River Thames and a lake in West Wales.   In the latter site they were particularly abundant in beds of the green alga *Chara*, but were also associated with stone surfaces and growths of freshwater sponge (Jenkins 1977).   It is obvious that more work on this species is needed before its habitat preferences can be described in any detail.

PSYCHOMYIIDAE

Our information about the habitat distribution of the Psychomyiidae derives mainly from the unpublished work of Alderson (1969) and the records collected by Jenkins (1977).   These studies relate principally to South Wales and further work is needed to discover whether the patterns described are of general occurrence.

In the streams and rivers of the uplands of South Wales the psychomyiids show a succession of species resembling that seen in the net-spinners. *Tinodes maclachlani* and *T. assimilis* are typically found in situations where small streams or seepages flow in thin films over vertical rock faces.   These rock faces often form the side walls of larger streams or rivers and correspond to the "hygropetric habitat" of continental workers (Vaillant 1953, 1954).   In the main channels of upland streams *T. dives* occupies the moorland headwaters but is replaced by *T. rostocki* where the stream flows through woodland (Alderson 1969).

T. waeneri appears downstream of these other two species.   Although *Psychomyia pusilla* may co-exist with *T. dives* in the headwaters, it also extends into larger streams and rivers (Alderson 1969, Jenkins 1977).

T. unicolor must be considered as something of a special case because of its association with highly calcareous waters.   All of the nineteen sites in South Wales where Alderson collected this species had a calcium content in excess of 60 mg l^{-1}.

Alderson (1969) argued that these patterns were related most directly to the distribution of algal communities, and probably only indirectly to physical variables.

Apparently interspecific competition may also play a part in determining distribution.   In lowland streams in South Wales where *T. dives* is absent, *T. maclachlani* extends its range from rock-face sites into the main channels of streams.

RHYACOPHILIDAE

Rhyacophila larvae are probably the caddis most restricted to conditions of high current-speed.   Their commitment to fast flow-rates reflects both the distribution of their food supply and their physiological limitations.   Philipson (1954) showed that in still water *R. dorsalis* was immobilized even at high oxygen concentration, and Ambühl (1959), working on *R. nubila*, found that the normal rate of oxygen consumption was not maintained when either water velocity or oxygen concentration was reduced.   It is significant that the larvae do not undulate the abdomen, as do those of Hydropsychidae and Polycentropodidae.   Such movements have a ventilatory function in the latter two families and their undulatory rate is increased under respiratory stress (Fox & Sidney 1953, Philipson 1954, 1978, Ambühl 1959, Philipson & Moorhouse 1974, 1976).

Scott (1958) found that *Rhyacophila* was most common in current-speeds of 80–90 cm s^{-1}.   He also found that *Rhyacophila dorsalis* was a frequent inhabitant of the mossy upper surfaces of stones.   On stones without moss the larvae were found only on the lower surfaces.   Dorier & Vaillant (1954) found *Rhyacophila* larvae in water velocities up to 125 cm s^{-1} in the field, and in the laboratory showed that larvae were not dislodged until the current speed reached 200 cm s^{-1}.

No detailed comparisons have been made of the habitats occupied by the four *Rhyacophila* species.

TABLE I. Available data on head capsule widths (mm) of caseless caddis of different instars.

Instar	1	2	3	4	5
Rhyacophila dorsalis	0·27–0·30	0·39–0·45	0·57–0·64	0·81–0·90	1·18–1·45
Rhyacophila munda	0·26–0·28	0·37–0·41	0·51–0·58	0·78–0·90	1·15–1·33
Polycentropus flavomaculatus	0·20	0·30–0·35	0·40–0·55	0·68–0·90	1·28–1·42
Polycentropus kingi	—	—	—	—	1·50–1·66
Plectrocnemia conspersa	0·25–0·40	0·45–0·70	0·80–1·10	1·30–1·75	1·85–2·70
Diplectrona felix	—	0·24–0·32	0·56–0·64	0·80–1·04	1·29–1·52
Hydropsyche fulvipes	—	—	—	—	1·72–1·76
Hydropsyche instabilis	—	0·26–0·32	0·56–0·64	0·88–1·04	1·44–1·74
Hydropsyche siltalai	0·20–0·22	0·24–0·35	0·43–0·68	0·78–1·15	1·42–1·71
Hydropsyche pellucidula	—	0·33–0·41	0·59–0·71	0·96–1·12	1·44–1·80
Hydropsyche contubernalis	—	—	—	0·80–0·96	1·28–1·60
Hydropsyche angustipennis	—	—	0·48–0·60	0·76–1·00	1·28–1·56
Cheumatopsyche lepida	—	—	—	—	0·92–0·96
Tinodes waeneri	0·15–0·20	0·23–0·27	0·33–0·43	0·45–0·59	0·71–0·85

LIFE HISTORIES

All the families considered here have basically similar life-history patterns. The adult female lays eggs in a plate-like mass, usually on a submerged boulder. After hatching, the larvae develop to maturity through a series of five instars. As with all insects, the change from one instar to the next involves a marked increase in size, and the progression of the population through successive instars can be monitored by making measurements of head-widths. The available information on head-widths for various species is set out in Table 1 (p. 75). The life cycle reconstructions given in Figures 141-152 have been made on this basis.

Fully developed (5th instar) larvae construct a stony pupal case. These pupal cases can be confused with the larval cases of case-bearing caddis. However, they differ from them in being firmly attached to stones and in having no obvious head opening. In some species, e.g. *Polycentropus flavomaculatus* and *Rhyacophila dorsalis*, 5th instar larvae occupy pupal cases during the winter and the pupal change is delayed until the following spring. Such larvae are usually referred to as resting larvae.

During the pupal period, which lasts about three weeks, the major structural changes necessary to produce the adult take place. Towards the end of this period, the adult genitalia are sufficiently well formed within the pupal skin to allow them to be used for identification purposes. This is useful because it also allows the identification of the last larval skin which remains in the pupal case.

Adult caddis are most frequently encountered in summer. A few species, however, have long flight-periods and occur in every month of the year except December and January. The pattern of emergence varies from one species to another and also, on a geographical basis, for any one species. Emergence patterns can be studied using emergence traps fixed over suitable habitats. Light-trap captures will also provide information about flight patterns but will not attract day-flying species such as *Diplectrona felix*.

A one-year life cycle is typical of the majority of species. The main variations occur when some individuals in a population require a second year to complete development, or where in favourable conditions a second generation can be completed within a single year.

Related species living in the same habitat often have staggered larval growth-periods. This may not be simply fortuitous and probably serves to

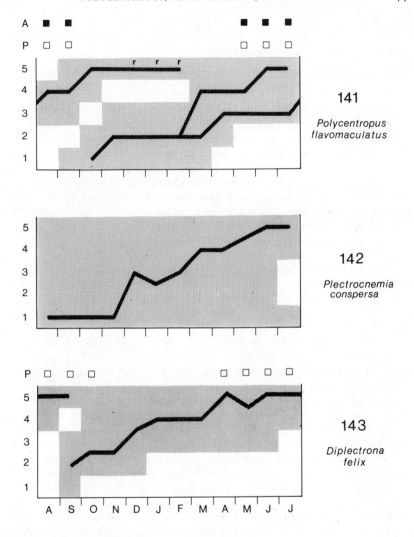

141

*Polycentropus
flavomaculatus*

142

*Plectrocnemia
conspersa*

143

*Diplectrona
felix*

Figs 141–143.   Life histories.
                Grey shading = monthly distribution of instars;
                thick line   = dominant instar group;
                r   = resting larvae;
                ■   = adults;
                □   = pupae (where recorded).
                (Fig. 141 after Elliott 1968).

reduce inter-specific competition.   Such species pairs include *Hydropsyche siltalai* and *H. pellucidula*; *Holocentropus picicornis* and *H. dubius*; *Psychomyia pusilla* and *Tinodes dives*.

POLYCENTROPODIDAE

The life cycle of *Polycentropus flavomaculatus* has been examined in detail by Elliott (1968) (Fig. 141).   Some larvae appear in the first instar in autumn and emerge as adults in the following summer.   Others, presumably derived from winter-hatching eggs, develop only as far as 3rd instar by July (lower trend-line in Fig. 141) and complete their growth in the following autumn.   These individuals overwinter as normal 5th instar larvae or "resting" larvae in pupal cases.   In this way, part of the population takes more than one year to complete its life cycle.   The widespread occurrence of two peaks of flight activity in light-trap captures suggests that this pattern is repeated throughout Great Britain (Crichton et al. 1978).

Little is known about the life histories of the localized species *Polycentropus irroratus* and *P. kingi*.   *P. kingi* has been taken in light traps in Wales (Crichton et al. 1978), where there was a single, well-defined, peak of flight activity in August.   Elliott (1968) took adults of this species in July, August and September.

In a study of *Plectrocnemia conspersa* in a small iron-rich stream in Sussex, evidence was obtained for a steady growth trend and a one-year life cycle, in spite of the fact that all instars were present for most of the year (Fig. 142).   The occurrence of 1st instar larvae in every monthly sample suggested that there was delayed hatching of some eggs.   The wide range of size groups may have the effect of decreasing competition, in view of the observed differences in diet between the various instars (Townsend & Hildrew 1978).

This pattern of larval development agrees with light-trap catches from Scotland and northern England, which showed an extended flight-period from May until October, with a single peak in late July and early August (Crichton et al. 1978).   In the south of England, however, there were two peaks of activity, one in late May and one in August.   Since Tachet (1967) has demonstrated in the laboratory that larvae hatching from eggs in April can give rise to adults in September, it seems that two broods a year are possible.   However this was clearly not the case in the iron-rich stream.

The flight-period of *P. geniculata* is from May to September, with a single July peak in Scotland and two peaks (June and August) in Wales and northern England (Crichton et al. 1978).   Jones (1969) has recorded its emergence from May to September in North Wales.

No detailed information on *Holocentropus* life cycles is available from Britain. However, Higler (1978) has described the pattern of larval growth of *H. picicornis* and *H. dubius* from a canal in the Netherlands. Small larvae of both species appeared in July, but *H. dubius* then grew more rapidly and overwintered at a larger size. Growth in *H. picicornis* accelerated in spring, and the pupation and emergence of the two species probably occurred at much the same time. It appears that all individuals of both species completed the life cycle in one year. This staggering of life cycles could be significant as a means of reducing competition between the two species.

Little information is available on the life cycles of the three *Cyrnus* species found in Britain. *Cyrnus trimaculatus* has a simple one-year life cycle in the River Thames and a single summer flight-period with a peak in July and August (Crichton et al. 1978). The flight activity began earlier (May) and finished later (September) in southern England than further north. *C. flavidus* has a single flight-period from July to September, with a peak in late July.

HYDROPSYCHIDAE

The life cycles of some British hydropsychids are well known. *Hydropsyche siltalai* has been studied in North Wales by Hynes (1961), on Dartmoor by Elliott (1968), in South Wales by Hildrew & Edington (1979), and in north-east England by Boon (1979). In all these areas the life cycle takes one year and there is a single flight-period. Figure 145 illustrates the life cycle of *H. siltalai* from the River Usk in South Wales. Hatching of eggs began in June and July and there was some growth of larvae until November, by which time most larvae were in the 3rd instar. Growth was rapid from March onwards and pupation began in June.

The life history of *H. pellucidula* is known from South Wales (Hildrew & Edington 1979) and from north-east England (Boon 1979) and differs markedly from that of *H. siltalai*. In the River Usk we found that, although emergence of *H. pellucidula* occurred only slightly earlier than that of *H. siltalai*, larval growth in the late summer was very rapid and the bulk of the population overwintered in the 5th instar (Fig. 144). Thus although *H. pellucidula* has a one-year development with a single extended flight-period, the life cycle is staggered compared with that of *H. siltalai*. The possible ecological significance of this is discussed by Hildrew (1978), Hildrew & Edington (1979) and Boon (1979).

It was found that the larval growth of *H. siltalai* in the River Usk (Hildrew 1978) and *H. pellucidula* in the North Tyne (Boon 1979) was accelerated in the lower reaches of these rivers.

In South Wales *H. instabilis* was found to have a pattern of growth and development very similar to *H. siltalai* (Hildrew & Edington 1979) (Fig. 146).

Monthly samples of *Diplectrona felix* larvae taken from a small wooded stream in South Wales suggested that a one-year life cycle was the normal pattern (Fig. 143), although a few individuals may have spent a second winter as 5th instar larvae. Daytime swarms of adults were observed in August. Jones (1969), using emergence traps in North Wales, recorded an emergence period from May until August with a peak in late June and early July. This species is not attracted to light traps.

Only fragmentary information is available on the life cycles of the remaining Hydropsychidae. Adults of *Hydropsyche angustipennis* in southern England were found to have a single flight-period from May to September with peak activity in late July (Crichton 1960, Crichton et al. 1978) although in Germany Matzdorf (1964) has recorded a double flight-period. Two flight-periods have also been recorded in *H. contubernalis* (Crichton et al. 1978), suggesting that the life cycle may be a complex one.

PHILOPOTAMIDAE

Very little can be said about philopotamid life cycles except that adult flight-periods seem to be very long in some species. Jones (1969) caught adults of *Wormaldia occipitalis* in North Wales in every month of the year except December and January, and Kimmins (1965) records *Philopotamus montanus* adults from April to September. Mackereth (1960) has suggested that *W. occipitalis* has a two-year life cycle in the Lake District.

ECNOMIDAE

Light-trap catches of *Ecnomus tenellus* in the south of England showed it to have a major peak of flight activity in July and a second smaller peak in late August (Crichton 1960, Crichton et al. 1978). A study of emerging adults by Jones (1976b) from a lake on Anglesey showed a single short emergence-period.

PSYCHOMYIIDAE

Most of our information about the life cycles of this family comes from unpublished work by Alderson (1969) and a study of *Tinodes waeneri* by Jones (1976a, b). Alderson found that in *T. dives* and *T. rostocki* development took one year (Figs 147, 148). Growth was continuous even during the winter months, and by January the population was dominated by 5th instar larvae. In the uplands of South Wales *Psychomyia pusilla* was also

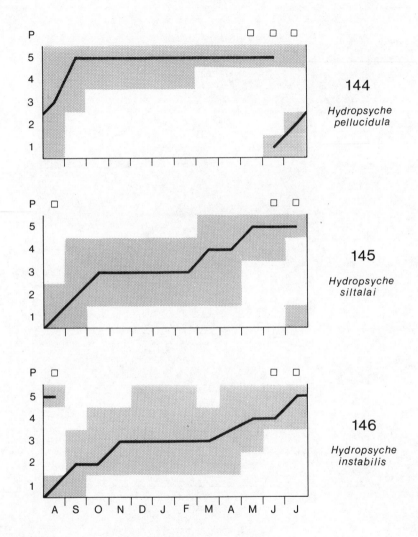

Figs 144–146.   Life histories.
Grey shading = monthly distribution of instars;
thick line   = dominant instar group;
□   = pupae.
(After Hildrew & Edington 1979).

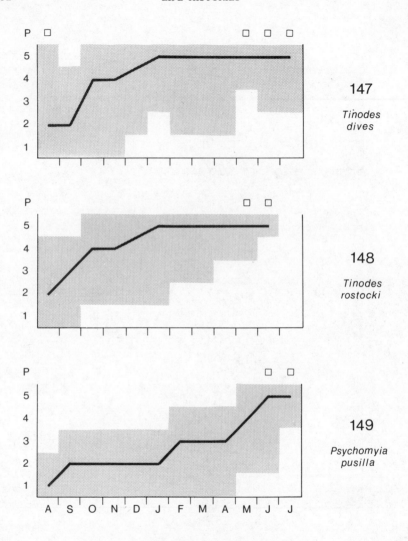

147

Tinodes dives

148

Tinodes rostocki

149

Psychomyia pusilla

Figs 147–149. Life histories.
Grey shading = monthly distribution of instars;
thick line   = dominant instar group;
□   = pupae.
(After Alderson 1969).

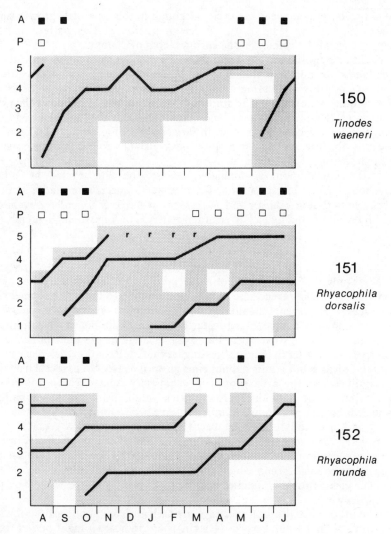

Figs 150–152. Life histories.
Grey shading = monthly distribution of instars;
thick line = dominant instar group;
r = resting larvae;
■ = adults;
□ = pupae.
(Fig. 150 after Jones 1976a; Figs 151, 152, after Elliott 1968).

found to have a one-year life cycle, although in this case little growth took place until spring (Fig. 149). Alderson attributed this pattern to the dependence of the species on the spring bloom of diatoms.

Light trap captures of *P. pusilla* showed a single peak of activity in July in Scotland. In northern England and Wales a second peak occurs in late August, possibly indicating two generations a year in these localities (Crichton et al. 1978). The study by Jones (1976a) of the larval growth pattern of *T. waeneri*, in a lowland lake in North Wales, strongly suggests that there is a second generation in late summer (Fig. 150). This would account for the double emergence peak usually found in this species (Crichton 1960, Crichton et al. 1978).

Little information is available about the life cycles of other psychomyiids. Alderson (1969) found that *T. maclachlani* had a similar life cycle to that of *T. dives* and *T. rostocki*, whereas *T. unicolor* grew more slowly in winter and had a late emergence period in August and September.

RHYACOPHILIDAE

The study by Elliott (1968) of *Rhyacophila dorsalis* indicated that most individuals (middle trend line in Fig. 151) completed their development in one year. However a smaller group, apparently hatching from eggs in winter, had grown only to 3rd instar by July and did not reach 5th instar until the following November (Fig. 151). These larvae built pupal cases but spent the winter in them as "resting larvae". Pupation took place from March onwards but adults did not emerge until May. In cases such as this it is unlikely that the larval groups are genetically isolated from one another, as variations in individual growth-rates would bring about exchanges between the groups. Adult *R. dorsalis* have been captured in light traps as early as April and late as November (Crichton et al. 1978).

Elliott (1968) has shown that *R. munda* has a similar life cycle, in the sense of including one larval group that completes its development in a year, and another small group which takes nearly two years (Fig. 152). This smaller group probably hatches from eggs in spring and overwinters as 4th instar larvae.

The life cycle of the local species *R. septentrionis* has not been described in Britain although adult records (Hickin 1967) indicate a flight period from June to September. *R. obliterata* has been taken in light traps between August and October in both England and Scotland, although the peak was about one month earlier in England. Hynes (1961) found that it overwintered as eggs or as 1st instar larvae.

ACKNOWLEDGEMENTS

We are grateful to the many people who have sent us material or have commented on earlier versions of the key. In the most recent phase of the work specimens provided by Dr J. P. O'Connor of the National Museum of Ireland and Mr R. A. Jenkins of the Welsh Water Authority have proved especially useful.

Our sections on the biology of the Psychomyiidae have drawn freely on the unpublished work of Dr R. Alderson and we are very grateful for his permission to use this material. We would also like to record our thanks to Mrs J. Mackereth for permission to reproduce the diagrams from her paper on *Rhyacophila* larvae, and to the Zoological Society of London, the Royal Entomological Society, Blackwell Scientific Publications and the editor of *Freshwater Biology* for permission to use diagrams originally published in their journals.

We would like to thank Professor D. Bellamy and Professor J. D. Pye for facilities at University College, Cardiff, and Queen Mary College, London, respectively. Finally we wish to acknowledge the assistance of Dr M. A. Edington throughout the course of the work and of Mrs C. Carrell in the preparation of the final manuscript.

REFERENCES

Alderson, R. (1969). Studies on the larval biology of caddis flies of the family Psychomyiidae. Unpublished Ph.D. Thesis, University of Wales.

Alm, G. (1926). Beiträge zur Kenntnis der netzspinnenden Trichopteren-Larven in Schweden. *Int. Revue ges. Hydrobiol. Hydrogr.* **14**, 233-275.

Ambühl, H. (1959). Die Bedeutung der Strömung als ökologischer Faktor. *Schweiz. Z. Hydrol.* **21**, 133-264.

Badcock, R. M. (1949). Studies on stream life in tributaries of the Welsh Dee. *J. Anim. Ecol.* **18**, 193-208.

Badcock, R. M. (1955). Widespread distribution in Britain of our allegedly rare caddis, *Hydropsyche fulvipes* (Curtis) (Trich., Hydropsychidae). *Entomologist's mon. Mag.* **91**, 30-31.

Badcock, R. M. (1975). The Hydropsychidae (Trichoptera) in Staffordshire. *N. Staffs. J. Field Stud.* **15**, 10-18.

Badcock, R. M. (1976). The distribution of the Hydropsychidae in Great Britain. In *Proc. 1st int. Symp. Trichoptera, 1974*, 49-58. The Hague. Junk.

Badcock, R. M. (1977). The *Hydropsyche fulvipes – instabilis – saxonica* (Trichoptera) complex in Britain and the recognition of *H. siltalai* Döhler. *Entomologist's mon. Mag.* **113**, 23-29.

Berg, K. (1938). Studies on the bottom animals of Esrom Lake. *K. danske Vidensk. Selsk. Skr.* **7**, 1-255.

Boon, P. J. (1978a). The pre-impoundment distribution of certain Trichoptera larvae in the North Tyne river system (Northern England), with particular reference to current speed. *Hydrobiologia* **57**, 167-174.

Boon, P. J. (1978b). The use of ventral sclerites in the taxonomy of larval hydropsychids. In *Proc. 2nd int. Symp. Trichoptera, 1977*, 165-173. The Hague. Junk.

Boon, P. J. (1979). Studies on the spatial and temporal distribution of larval Hydropsychidae in the North Tyne river system (Northern England). *Arch. Hydrobiol.* **85**, 336-359.

Brickenstein, C. (1955). Über die Netzbau der Larve von *Neureclipsis bimaculata* (L). *Abh. bayer. Akad. Wiss.* **69**, 1-44.

Crichton, M. I. (1960). A study of captures of Trichoptera in a light trap near Reading, Berkshire. *Trans. R. ent. Soc. Lond.* **112**, 319-344.

Crichton, M. I., Fisher, D. & Woiwood, I. P. (1978). Life histories and distribution of British Trichoptera, excluding Limnephilidae and Hydroptilidae, based on the Rothamsted Insect Survey. *Holarct. Ecol.* **1**, 31-45.

Danecker, E. (1961). Studien zur hygropetrischen Fauna. Biologie und Ökologie von *Stactobia* und *Tinodes*. *Int. Revue ges. Hydrobiol. Hydrogr.* **46**, 214-254.

Décamps, H. (1968). Vicariances écologiques chez les trichoptères des Pyrénées. *Annls Limnol.* **4,** 1-50.

Dorier, A. & Vaillant, F. (1954). Observations et expériences relatives à la résistance au courant de divers invertébrés aquatiques. *Trav. Lab. Hydrobiol. Piscic. Univ. Grenoble,* **45 & 46,** 9-31.

Dunn, D. R. (1954). The feeding habits of some of the fishes and some members of the bottom fauna of Llyn Tegid (Bala Lake) Merionethshire. *J. Anim. Ecol.* **23,** 224-233.

Edington, J. M. (1964). The taxonomy of British polycentropid larvae (Trichoptera). *Proc. zool. Soc. Lond.* **143,** 281-300.

Edington, J. M. (1965). The effect of water flow on populations of net-spinning Trichoptera. *Mitt. int. Verein. theor. angew. Limnol.* **13,** 40-48.

Edington, J. M. (1968). Habitat preferences in net-spinning caddis larvae with special reference to the influence of water velocity. *J. Anim. Ecol.* **37,** 675-692.

Edington, J. M. & Alderson, R. (1973). The taxonomy of British psychomyiid larvae (Trichoptera). *Freshwat. Biol.* **3,** 463-478.

Edington, J. M. & Hildrew, A. G. (1973). Experimental observations relating to the distribution of net-spinning Trichoptera in streams. *Verh. int. Verein. theor. angew. Limnol.* **18,** 1549-1558.

Elliott, J. M. (1968). The life histories and drifting of Trichoptera in a Dartmoor stream. *J. Anim. Ecol.* **37,** 615-625.

Fisher, D. (1977). Identification of adult females of *Tinodes* in Britain (Trichoptera: Psychomyiidae). *Syst. Ent.* **2,** 105-110.

Fox, H. M. & Sidney, J. (1953). Influence of dissolved oxygen on the respiratory movements of caddis larvae. *J. exp. Biol.* **30,** 235-237.

Fox, P. J. (1978). Caddis larvae (Trichoptera) as predators of fish eggs. *Freshwat. Biol.* **8,** 343-345.

Fritsch, F. E. (1950). *Phormidium incrustatum* (Naeg.) Gom., an important member of the lime encrusted communities of flowing water. *Biol. Jaarb.* **70,** 27-39.

Hickin, N. E. (1950). Larvae of the British Trichoptera, 30. *Tinodes pallidula* McLachlan (Psychomyiidae). *Proc. R. ent. Soc. Lond. (A)* **25,** 103-106.

Hickin, N. E. (1953). *Tinodes pallidula* McLachlan (Trichoptera, Psychomyiidae). A second British station. *Entomologist* **86,** 113.

Hickin, N. E. (1954). Larvae of the British Trichoptera, 42. *Rhyacophila septentrionis* McLachlan (Rhyacophilidae). *Proc. R. ent. Soc. Lond. (A)* **29,** 59-61.

Hickin, N. E. (1967). *Caddis larvae. Larvae of the British Trichoptera.* London. Hutchinson. 476 pp.

Higler, L. W. G. (1978). Observations on caddis larvae in *Stratiotes* vegetation. In *Proc. 2nd int. Symp. Trichoptera, 1977,* 309-315. The Hague. Junk.

Hildrew, A. G. (1978). Ecological aspects of life history in some net-spinning Trichoptera. In *Proc. 2nd int. Symp. Trichoptera, 1977,* 269-281. The Hague. Junk.

Hildrew, A. G. & Edington, J. M. (1979).   Factors facilitating the coexistence of hydropsychid caddis larvae in the same river system. *J. Anim. Ecol.* **48**, 557-576.
Hildrew, A. G. & Morgan, J. C. (1974).   The taxonomy of the British Hydropsychidae (Trichoptera). *J. Ent. (B)* **43**, 217-229.
Hildrew, A. G. & Townsend, C. R. (1976).   The distribution of two predators and their prey in an iron-rich stream. *J. Anim. Ecol.* **45**, 41-57.
Hildrew, A. G. & Townsend, C. R. (1980).   Aggregation, interference and foraging by larvae of *Plectrocnemia conspersa* (Trichoptera: Poly-centropodidae). *Anim. Behav.* **28**, 553-560.
Hynes, H. B. N. (1961).   The invertebrate fauna of a Welsh mountain stream. *Arch. Hydrobiol.* **57**, 344-388.
Jansson, A. & Vuoristo, T. (1979).   Significance of stridulation in larval Hydropsychidae (Trichoptera). *Behaviour* **71**, 168-186.
Jenkins, R. A. (1977).   Notes on the distribution of psychomyiid larvae (Trichoptera) in South-West Wales. *Entomologist's Rec. J. Var.* **89**, 57-61.
Johnstone, G. W. (1964).   Stridulation by larval Hydropsychidae. *Proc. R. ent. Soc. Lond. (A)* **39**, 146-150.
Jones, J. R. E. (1949).   A further ecological study of the calcareous streams in the 'Black Mountain' district of South Wales. *J. Anim. Ecol.* **18**, 142-159.
Jones, J. R. E. (1950).   A further ecological study of the River Rheidol; the food of the common insects of the main-stream. *J. Anim. Ecol.* **19**, 159-174.
Jones, N. V. (1969).   The emergence of Trichoptera from a small ground-fed stream in North Wales. *Entomologist's mon. Mag.* **105**, 151-155.
Jones, N. V. (1976a).   The Trichoptera of the stony shore of a lake with particular reference to *Tinodes waeneri* (L.) (Psychomyiidae). In *Proc. 1st int. Symp. Trichoptera, 1974*, 117-130. The Hague. Junk.
Jones, N. V. (1976b).   Studies on the eggs, larvae and pupae of *Tinodes waeneri* (L.). In *Proc. 1st int. Symp. Trichoptera, 1974*, 131-143. The Hague. Junk.
Kaiser, P. (1965).   Über Netzbau und Strömungssinn bei den Larven der Gattung *Hydropsyche* Pict. (Ins. Trichoptera). *Int. Revue ges. Hydrobiol. Hydrogr.* **50**, 169-224.
Kimmins, D. E. (1942).   *Cyrnus insolutus* McL. (Trichoptera), new to Britain. *Entomologist* **75**, 66-68.
Kimmins, D. E. (1949).   *Tinodes pallidula* McLachlan: an addition to the British list of Trichoptera. *Entomologist* **82**, 269-272.
Kimmins, D. E. (1953).   A key to the European species of *Wormaldia*, with descriptions of two new species. *Ann. Mag. nat. Hist.* **6**, 801-808.
Kimmins, D. E. (1965).   Keys to the British species of Rhyacophilidae and Philopotamidae. *Entomologist's Gaz.* **16**, 147-161.
Kimmins, D. E. (1966).   A revised checklist of the British Trichoptera. *Entomologist's Gaz.* **17**, 111-120.
Krawany, H. (1930).   Trichopteren-Studien im Gebiet der Lunzer Seen. *Int. Revue ges. Hydrobiol. Hydrogr.* **23**, 417-427.

Lepneva, S. G. (1956). Morphological relationships of the subfamilies Psychomyiinae, Ecnominae and Polycentropinae (Trichoptera) in the preimaginal stages. *Ent. Obozr.* **35,** 8-27. (In Russian).

Lepneva, S. G. (1970). *Fauna of the U.S.S.R. Trichoptera 1, Larvae and Pupae of Annulipalpia.* Translation from 1964 Russian edition. Jerusalem. Israel Program for Scientific Translations.

Macan, T. T. (1973). A key to the adults of the British Trichoptera. *Scient. Publs. Freshwat. Biol. Ass.* **28,** 1-151.

Mackereth, J. C. (1954). Taxonomy of the British species of the genus *Rhyacophila* (Trichoptera). *Proc. R. ent. Soc. Lond. (A)* **29,** 147-152.

Mackereth, J. C. (1960). Notes on the Trichoptera of a stony stream. *Proc. R. ent. Soc. Lond. (A)* **35,** 17-23.

Malas, D. & Wallace, J. B. (1977). Strategies for coexistence in three species of net-spinning caddis flies (Trichoptera) in second-order Southern Appalachian streams. *Can. J. Zool.* **55,** 1829-1840.

Malicky, H. (1977). Ein Beitrag zur Kenntnis der *Hydropsyche guttata* – Gruppe (Trichoptera, Hydropsychidae). *Z. ArbGem. Öst. Ent.* **29,** 1-28.

Marshall, J. E. (1978). Trichoptera: Hydroptilidae. *Handbk Ident. Br. Insects* **1,** 14(a), 1-31.

Matzdorf, F. (1964). Beitrag zur Biologie von *Hydropsyche angustipennis* Curtis (Trich.). *Ent. Ber., Berlin* **2,** 73-79.

Mosely, M. E. (1939). *The British caddis flies (Trichoptera).* London. Routledge. 320 pp.

Nielsen, A. (1942). Über die Entwicklung und Biologie der Trichopteren mit besonderer Berücksichtigung der Quelltrichopteren Himmerlands. *Arch. Hydrobiol. (Suppl.)* **17,** 255-631.

Nielsen, A. (1948). Postembryonic development of the Hydroptilidae. *Biol. Skr.* **5,** 1-200.

O'Connor, J. P. (1977). Lough Derrygeeha, Co. Clare, a new locality for *Cyrnus insolutus* McLachlan (Trichoptera: Polycentropodidae). *Entomologist's Rec. J. Var.* **89,** 309-310.

O'Connor, J. P. & Wise, E. J. (1980). Larva of *Tinodes maculicornis* (Pictet) (Trichoptera: Psychomyiidae) with notes on the species' distribution and habitat in Ireland. *Freshwat. Biol.* **10,** 367-370.

Percival, E. & Whitehead, H. (1929). A quantitative study of the fauna of some types of stream-bed. *J. Ecol.* **17,** 282-314.

Philipson, G. N. (1953a). The larva and pupa of *Hydropsyche instabilis* Curtis (Trichoptera, Hydropsychidae). *Proc. R. ent. Soc. Lond. (A)* **28,** 17-23.

Philipson, G. N. (1953b). The larva and pupa of *Wormaldia subnigra* (McLachlan) (Trichoptera, Philopotamidae). *Proc. R. ent. Soc. Lond. (A)* **28,** 57-62.

Philipson, G. N. (1954). The effect of water flow and oxygen concentration on six species of caddis fly (Trichoptera) larvae. *Proc. zool. Soc. Lond.* **124,** 547-564.

Philipson, G. N. (1957). Records of caddis flies (Trichoptera) in Northumberland with notes on their seasonal distribution in Plessey Woods. *Trans. nat. Hist. Soc. Northumb.* **12,** 77-92.

Philipson, G. N. (1969).   Some factors affecting the net-spinning of the caddis fly *Hydropsyche instabilis* Curtis (Trichoptera: Hydropsychidae). *Hydrobiologia* **34,** 369-377.

Philipson, G. N. (1978).   The undulatory behaviour of larvae of *Hydropsyche pellucidula* Curtis and *Hydropsyche siltalai* Döhler.   In *Proc. 2nd int. Symp. Trichoptera, 1977,* 241-247.   The Hague.   Junk.

Philipson, G. N. & Moorhouse, B. H. S. (1974).   Observations on ventilatory and net-spinning activities of the larvae of the genus *Hydropsyche* Pictet (Trichoptera: Hydropsychidae) under experimental conditions.   *Freshwat. Biol.* **4,** 525-533.

Philipson, G. N. & Moorhouse, B. H. S. (1976).   Respiratory behaviour of larvae of four species of the family Polycentropodidae (Trichoptera). *Freshwat. Biol.* **6,** 347-353.

Ruttner, F. (1963).   *Fundamendals of limnology.* 3rd edn. Toronto. University of Toronto Press. 295 pp.

Sattler, W. (1958).   Beiträge zur Kenntnis von Lebensweise und Körperbau der Larve und Puppe von *Hydropsyche* Pict. (Trichoptera) mit besonderer Berücksichtigung des Netzbaues. *Z. Morph. Ökol. Tiere* **47,** 115-192.

Sattler, W. (1963).   Über den Körperbau und Ethologie der Larve und Puppe von *Macronema* Pict. (Hydropsychidae), ein als Larve sich von 'Mikro-Drift' ernährendes Trichopter aus dem Amazongebiet. *Arch. Hydrobiol.* **59,** 26-60.

Schumacher, H. (1970).   Untersuchungen zur Taxonomie, Biologie und Ökologie einiger Köcherfliegenarten der Gattung *Hydropsyche* Pict. (Insecta, Trichoptera). *Int. Revue ges. Hydrobiol. Hydrogr.* **55,** 511-557.

Scott, D. (1958).   Ecological studies on the Trichoptera of the River Dean, Cheshire. *Arch. Hydrobiol.* **54,** 340-392.

Sedlák, E. (1971).   Bestimmungstabelle der Larven der Häufigen Tschechoslowakischen Arten der Gattung *Hydropsyche* Pictet (Trichoptera). *Acta ent. bohemoslav.* **68,** 185-187.

Siltala, A. J. (1907).   Über die Nahrung der Trichopteren. *Acta Soc. Flora Fauna fenn.* **29,** 1-34.

Silver, S. C. (1980).   Ultrasound production during stridulation by hydropsychid larvae (Trichoptera). *J. Zool.* **191,** 323-331.

Slack, H. D. (1936).   The food of the caddis fly (Trichoptera) larvae. *J. Anim. Ecol.* **5,** 105-115.

Tachet, H. (1965).   Récherches sur l'alimentation des larves de *Polycentropus* (Trichoptère) dans leur milieu naturel. *Annls Soc. ent. Fr.* NS, **1,** 627-633.

Tachet, H. (1967).   Quelques aspects du cycle biologique de *Plectrocnemia conspersa* (Curtis 1834) (Trichoptera, Polycentropodidae). *Annls Limnol.* **3,** 177-184.

Tachet, H. (1971a).   Le filet-piège de la larve de *Plectrocnemia conspersa* (Trichoptères, Polycentropodidae). *Oecologia* **8,** 78-92.

Tachet, H. (1971b).   Aspects descriptifs du comportement alimentaire chez la larve de *Plectrocnemia conspersa* (Trichoptera, Polycentropodidae). *Z. Tierpsychol.* **28,** 175-184.

Tachet, H. (1977). Vibrations and predatory behaviour of *Plectrocnemia* larvae (Trichoptera). *Z. Tierpsychol.* **45**, 61-74.

Tobias, W. (1972a). Zur Kenntnis europäischer Hydropsychidae (Insecta: Trichoptera) I. *Senckenberg. biol.* **53**, 59-89.

Tobias, W. (1972b). Zur Kenntnis europäischer Hydropsychidae (Insecta: Trichoptera) II. *Senckenberg. biol.* **53**, 245-268.

Townsend, C. R. & Hildrew, A. G. (1978). Predation strategy and resource utilization by *Plectrocnemia conspersa* (Curtis) (Trichoptera: Polycentropodidae). In *Proc. 2nd int. Symp. Trichoptera, 1977,* 283-291. The Hague. Junk.

Townsend, C. R. & Hildrew, A. G. (1979). Form and function of the prey catching net of *Plectrocnemia conspersa* (Curtis) larvae (Trichoptera: Polycentropodidae). *Oikos* **33**, 412-418.

Vaillant, F. (1953). Les Trichoptères à larves hygropétriques. *Trav. Lab. Hydrobiol. Piscic. Univ. Grenoble* **45**, 33-48.

Vaillant, F. (1954). *Tinodes algirica* McLachlan, the hygropetric larvae of the *Tinodes* (Trichoptera). *Ann. Mag. nat. Hist.* **7**, 58-62.

Wallace, J. B. (1975). Food partitioning in net-spinning Trichoptera larvae: *Hydropsyche venularis, Cheumatopsyche etrona* and *Macronema zebratum* (Hydropsychidae). *Ann. ent. Soc. Am.* **68**, 463-472.

Wallace, J. B. & Malas, D. (1976). The fine structure of capture nets of larval Philopotamidae (Trichoptera): with special emphasis on *Dolophilodes distinctus. Can. J. Zool.* **54**, 1788-1802.

Wallace, J. B. & Merritt, R. W. (1980). Filter-feeding ecology of aquatic insects. *A. Rev. Ent.* **25**, 103-132.

Wallace, J. B., Webster, J. R. & Woodall, W. R. (1977). Role of filter feeders in flowing waters. *Arch. Hydrobiol.* **79**, 506-532.

Wesenberg-Lund, C. (1911). Biologische studien über den netzspinnende Trichopteren larven. *Int. Revue ges. Hydrobiol. Hydrogr.* (Biol. Suppl.) **3**, 1-64.

Wiggins, G. B. (1977). *Larvae of the North American caddis fly genera (Trichoptera).* Toronto. University of Toronto Press. 401 pp.

Williams, N. E. & Hynes, H. B. N. (1973). Microdistribution and feeding of the net-spinning caddis flies (Trichoptera) of a Canadian stream. *Oikos* **24**, 73-84.

INDEX

Page numbers in **bold** type refer to taxonomic aspects, those in plain type refer to ecological aspects. Redundant specific names are shown in parentheses.